JONATHANREA

MY AUTOBIOGRAPHY DREAM. BELIEVE. ACHIEVE.

JONATHANREA

MY AUTOBIOGRAPHY DREAM. BELIEVE. ACHIEVE.

FOREWORD BY CARL FOGARTY

HarperCollins*Publishers*

HarperCollins*Publishers*
1 London Bridge Street
London SE1 9GF

www.harpercollins.co.uk

First published by HarperCollins*Publishers* 2018
This updated edition 2019

1 3 5 7 9 10 8 6 4 2

A catalogue record of this book is
available from the British Library

ISBN 978-0-00-830510-9

All photos courtesy of the author, with the following exceptions:

p 2 (bottom right), p 3 (bottom), p 4 (all), p 6 (all) © Double Red
Photographic; p 5, p 7 (top, bottom left), p 9 (bottom), p 10 (all), p 11 (all),
p 12 (centre right), p 13 (centre right), p 14 (bottom right), p 16 (top, bottom
left) © Graeme Brown/GeeBee Images; p 7 (centre) © Alex Chailan;
p 7 (bottom right) © Graeme Brown/2Snap; p 9 (top) © Frozenspeed
Motorsport Photography; p 12 (bottom) © Kawasaki Heavy Industries;
p 13 (top left) © Matt Mackey; p 14 (centre left) © Ian Cairns; p 15 (top
left) © Press Eye/IFA; p 16 (centre) © Kevin Cringle

Printed and bound in Great Britain by
CPI Group (UK) Ltd, Croydon, CR0 4YY

MIX
Paper from
responsible sources
FSC™ C007454

For Tatia, Jake and Tyler

CONTENTS

FOREWORD

By Carl Fogarty

MY FIRST CONNECTION with the Rea family was more than four decades ago in 1977 when my dad, George, finished second behind Joey Dunlop in his first TT victory on the Rea Racing Yamaha sponsored by Jonathan's grandad, John.

John Rea was a jovial Irishman who loved his racing, and I was a bit in awe of him when I first met him for my debut at the 1987 North West 200 and he gave me some words of encouragement. The family connections continued when I raced on the roads against Jonathan's dad, Johnny. I was fourth on the bike I borrowed for the Junior race in 1989, when Johnny claimed his only TT win.

Many years later, Jonathan was one of a number of up-and-coming British lads, along with the likes of Leon Camier, Cal Crutchlow and Tom Sykes, who my Foggy Petronas Racing team considered for our final year in World Superbikes in 2006, before we finally opted for the late Craig Jones.

I don't remember speaking to Jonathan until I answered a call from an unknown number when staggering out of a beach club in Marbella, after a couple too many shandies. He was racing for HM Plant in the British Superbike Championship in 2007 and had just received an offer from Ducati to compete in the World Superbike Championship the following year. You had to respect the lad's confidence for calling me up out of the blue. I told him that the Ducati team manager, Davide Tardozzi, would look after him and that he should take the offer. He obviously didn't listen to a word I said, because he signed for Ten Kate Honda!

Within a couple of years, I was convinced that he was the fastest, most talented guy in the World Superbike Championship. But, relatively new to the class, he was a bit inconsistent, which was to be expected. His career mirrored mine in a lot of ways – I had to prove myself in a team and on a bike that were not the best out there. A few people started to doubt what I was saying about him, but I told them to be patient. The best rider nearly always ends up with the best package, and that happened to Jonathan, too, when he signed for Kawasaki.

The rest is history – including my record number of 59 wins! I'm often asked how that feels and the honest answer is that, if I had to lose the record to anyone, I couldn't be happier that it was Jonathan who beat it. Family connections aside, there is nobody more talented, more determined or more deserving, and there isn't a box that he doesn't tick for me. He's also a genuinely good guy, a proud family man who doesn't have an arrogant bone in his body. And, not content with beating my records, he even had the cheek to try to sell more books than me by asking me to write this Foreword.

Dream on, mate! :) #1

PROLOGUE

I'M NOT CRAZY

I'VE BEEN KNOCKED out more times than I can remember ... I have a separated acromioclavicular joint in my shoulder ... I've had a broken left collarbone, two broken ribs, two scapholunate wrist reconstructions (left and right) ... a broken right radius, two bad breaks of my left femur (one compound, one very complicated) ... a complete reconstruction of the medial collateral ligament and anterior cruciate ligaments in my left knee and an ACL reconstruction in the right ... a broken right tibia and fibula, a broken left ankle and a few broken metatarsals. Worst by far are my knees: they're in really bad shape, especially the right one.

I've had the end of my finger worn down to the bone. And I've been told I'd never ride a motorbike again, let alone race one.

I didn't listen, though.

This list is nothing unusual and I'm not complaining, it's just the price I pay to do the sport I love. From head to toe, my body has paid its dues.

'You must be mad.' ... *'Racers are crazy.'* ... *'You must take your brains out before you put your helmet on.'*

Listen. I am not crazy.

Focused? Yes.

Selfish? Of course.

Driven? For sure.

But a crazy thrill-seeker? You don't understand me or my sport.

I've been riding since I was two, racing since I was six. At the time of writing, I've been crowned World Superbike Champion three times, scored the most points ever in a single SBK season and won the Suzuka 8 Hours endurance race. I've ridden in one British Supersport season, three British Superbike, one World Supersport and ten SBK championships so far. And I'm pretty far from being done.

This is an elite sport. You have to be very, very clever and very, very fit. You win by working margins in the thousandths of a second. You throw a 165kg motorcycle from side to side, guide it as fast as possible around tight turns, brake hard and late while fighting G-forces and intense winds. It can and does go wrong, with devastating physical and emotional consequences. But I don't see anything reckless or crazy in risking that. Do you?

I see it as a true sport and sometimes even an art form in trying to get it right, to keep aiming for perfection.

They say racing is like a drug, but I've lived quite a clean life, so I can't really say. I know racing is a bug that bit me young and has not let go.

And I know that winning is what drives me.

That means, yes, I am selfish. Every elite sport demands levels of sacrifice and commitment that are hard to imagine from the outside. Endless training and preparation and thinking and rethinking. Countless days and weeks in hospitals and months in rehab.

Any rider who has reached the top has travelled a long and bumpy road, marred by serious injury and, in some cases, worse. Having a family now, it has become harder. I'm responsible for my wife Tatia and our boys Jake and Tyler. And while this is my lifelong dream and my overriding passion, I do understand it's not theirs.

I get nervous on the grid, but not about getting hurt. I focus on the perfect start, nothing else. I never think 'What if I crash?', 'What if my brakes don't work?' or 'What if I get hit by another rider?' You never think it's going to be you.

Yes, I'm very selfish and self-driven. No, I never think about the dark side or the dangers. That's my racer's brain. I park an emotion and I move on.

Shall we move on?

CHAPTER 1

SIXTY

Saturday, 9 June 2018, Automotodrom Brno, Czech Republic

The stress levels are at maximum now.

At the very last moment, just as I roll to a stop, I find neutral. I give Uri a gentle nod, because he's always as stressed as I am about me finding it. I turn back to the start lights and do a couple of nervous twitches with my head, something that's developed over the last few years. All the other riders are in position. The start marshal walks off, pointing his red flag towards the lights. We wait. Those lights will come on for anything between two and five seconds. As soon as they go out, it's a start. I engage first gear and activate launch control.

The lights come on, I twist the throttle. The decibel level soars as the other riders do the same. One ... two ... three ... four ...

It's race day.

This morning I qualified second fastest in the Superpole session – the middle of the front row of the grid. The whole post-Superpole parc fermé thing, photographs and inter-views, is dragging on. It's less than two hours from the lights going out for the 1pm race. I'm thinking I need some food and quiet time.

What I am definitely not thinking is this: I'm not thinking I could be breaking a record today. Sixty doesn't enter my mind.

I run back to my race truck office where my personal assistant Kevin Havenhand has picked up some grilled chicken and broccoli. I've not eaten since breakfast and I need to get this down now so I'm not bloated for the race. I scoff it while getting changed and watching the qualifying sessions for one of the support classes, Supersport 300, but I don't eat much – just enough so I don't feel hungry later. I stay in the truck while the physio checks my ankle, which has been hurting the last couple of days. My riding coach, Fabien Foret, is running through final details about the race and my plan of attack. He leaves and switches off the lights and I roll out a mat on the floor and rest my head on a team jacket. I'm out like a light.

The alarm goes off a quarter of an hour later, around ten past twelve, which gives me another 15 minutes to get ready. Kev has got a fresh, clean inner suit ready and all my riding gear is lined up in neat rows, just how I like it. I hop on the scales – a normal 71.3kg. Albert's back in to log my weight and apply some Kinesio therapeutic tape to my arms. I had some arm-pump problems at the previous round – 'carpal tunnel syndrome' caused by heavy braking and the constant pressure and vibration. It can cause numbness and tingling, and it's bloody painful; but that was mostly down to the nature of the Donington Park circuit and I've had no problems here at Brno, so this is just a precaution. As soon as that's done, I finish climbing into my leathers and me, Kev and Fab are marching out of the office like the Three Musketeers.

We know that we have the pace to win here – I've been fastest in all the longer runs we've done in practice – so strangely this is one of the tougher weekends mentally. I'm starting from the front row and I know I'm faster than everyone else, so the only person who can mess it up is me.

Fab reminds me of that and talks about the initial plan for the race: relax, get into a rhythm and see how the first few laps pan out. If I'm in front, I'll do a five-lap attack, put my head down, try to build a lead and manage the race from there.

What is it they say about battle plans? None of them survives first contact with the enemy …

I've been nervous since I started changing. I've got that familiar feeling of knotted tension in my stomach as adrenalin begins to flow around my body and it subconsciously prepares for fight or flight (or maybe both).

One minute, I'm focusing on my getaway, needing it to be clean and fast. The next, I'm wondering who is going to be challenging me this afternoon. It could be Marco Melandri, lining up to my right on the front row. He's shown some pace. Or it could be my team-mate Tom Sykes, on the other side in pole position.

Mostly, I'm starting to focus on winning. Only winning. It's the reason I'm here, it's the thing I'm paid to do.

It's 12.25pm and I'm on my chair in the garage, waiting for the pit-lane to open at 12.40, running through a few last-minute details with my crew chief, Pere Riba, who is confirming which tyres we're using and whether he's made any final changes to the bike. We're rolling into the race with the exact same bike we had in Superpole. I give my mechanics a tiny nod and they whip off the tyre warmers – little electric blankets that keep the tyres ready at around 90°C.

The Kawasaki ZX-10R is fired up and we're out on the sighting lap, once around the circuit and back to form up on the grid. I take in the crowd, especially in the stadium section – a series of four corners with a massive grassy bank off to the right, a great place to watch. There was quite a crowd during this morning's sessions, already on the beer and enjoying the Czech hospitality, so they're pretty noisy by now. I see quite a few Northern Ireland flags as well – hello, boys.

I roll up to the front row of the grid where the crew take off my gloves and helmet. I point out to Pere that the brakes are binding a little but everything else is OK. The brakes thing is nothing major, and the guys are on it straight away, but I'm particularly sensitive to it today. Must be the adrenalin.

The nerves are really kicking in. They've been building since I was changing, and they make my breathing a little shorter and my mouth quite dry. I'm hydrating often, without thinking; it's instinctive now.

I'm aware of a Monster Energy grid girl on my left and a Pirelli 'Best Lap' girl on the right. I've got the highest number of fastest laps this season and she's there for a PR opportunity with the official tyre supplier in front of the TV cameras on the grid. But my nerves are playing hell with my bladder and I'm busting for a piss, so I ruin the TV moment by running off the grid towards a toilet at the bottom of the race control tower.

In previous years, if I was caught short I'd have a piss at the side of the grid. The organisers didn't like it though – too close to sponsor banners – and if I do it again I'll be fined €5,000.

When I get back, everyone's quiet and focused – very few words from the mechanics or me. Two TV crews come over for an interview. The first is from Austria, simple questions about the race; the second is British Eurosport and their reporter Charlie Hiscott, who starts asking when I'm going to decide who I'll ride for next season.

He asks if I have a plan, so I tell him the only plan I'm thinking about right now is getting on with this race.

The five-minute board goes up and, because I always like to have my helmet and gloves on before the three-minute board, I take off my cap and sunglasses and hand them to Kev, who's standing just to my right. The air temperature is around 26°C, so I rub my face and hands with a cool damp towel. I pull on my Arai, tighten the D-ring strap and bring down the visor about halfway, then push my hands into my

Alpinestars gloves. As the three-minute board goes up, most of the team give me a pat, or a thumbs-up, and head off the grid, leaving just me and my two mechanics – Uri, who looks after the tyre warmer and bike stand at the front, and Arturo, who takes care of the rear. Uri stands there beside me and gently rubs his hand up and down the outside of my thigh.

He and I are quite connected, almost subconsciously. Maybe that's why we never talk about the fact that he stands there and rubs my leg during those last few minutes on the grid. But because I'm so nervous it's strangely comforting, knowing someone's there with me as I'm just staring at the dashboard, trying to visualise the perfect start. With about one minute and thirty seconds to go, Uri flicks the ignition on and starts the bike and, as the final one-minute board goes up, the tyre warmers come off, the bike is taken off its stands and I get a homie-style hand shake from Uri.

'*Vamos*,' he says. 'Let's go.' Arturo does the same, but with no words, and off they both go. It's me and the bike, and 18 laps of Brno.

Then we get a green flag to start the warm-up lap.

I put my left foot under the gear-shift lever and click it up to select first gear (the gearbox has a race shift pattern, the opposite to a road bike).

I accelerate away from the start line and push down on the lever to select second, again for third.

Then we're braking for the first corner and I'm nudging the lever up to go back down a gear.

I always do a fast warm-up lap and get back to the grid quickly to give myself a few extra seconds. As I come out of

Brno's final corner, I accelerate hard in second gear and then start giving the lever the gentlest nudge upwards as I roll towards my grid position, struggling to find neutral.

I've suffered from false neutrals in the past – when the gearbox finds neutral instead of engaging the gear you want – so my team has deliberately made it difficult to find.

I need to find it for the start of a race because, when I click into first gear immediately after neutral, the bike's electronic launch control system is automatically engaged.

I hold the throttle wide-open, and it sets the rpm at the right level in the torque range to maximise acceleration. I feed out the clutch to launch the bike, then I have to adjust the throttle slightly to try to keep the engine in the same rpm range. It's a fine art, but at the end of virtually every session I do a practice start and it's something I've mastered over the years.

At the same time, there's another part of the launch control that prevents the front wheel going up in the air as I pull away from the line. But the possibility of not finding neutral before the start always makes me even more anxious.

Then I find it, and I give Uri that nod and the starting lights go on.

One … two … three … four …

The lights take four seconds to go out and we're away, eyes focused on the turn-in point for the first corner, about 450m down the track.

My start is perfect, and, with a power-to-weight ratio not far off that of an F1 car, the acceleration is amazing.

I see nothing but the track ahead, no other bikes in my peripheral vision, although I know they're there.

I hit my braking marker and sit up from behind the bubble of the screen as my right index finger squeezes the brake lever.

My head and chest are slammed by the force of the wind that's trying to blow me off the back of the bike, which is itself pitching forward under the brakes.

I don't know how much force is going through my arms and wrists – in both directions as I'm hanging on to the handlebars – but it feels like a lot.

I move my right butt cheek off the seat and prepare to tip into the right-hander, leaning the bike over to counter the centrifugal forces that want to send both it and me in the opposite direction.

I lead into the long 180° first corner and extend my right knee outwards until the plastic knee-slider is skimming the kerb, telling me how far the bike is leant over.

This is when the tyres do their thing, the sticky, treadless rubber preventing the bike from sliding out from underneath me through a contact patch on the tarmac about the size of a credit card.

Coming out of the corner, I pick the bike up, shift myself back into a central position and put my head back down behind the screen. I'm accelerating hard towards the little left kink that is turn two and then off to turns three and four, a tight left followed quickly by a slightly more open right, like a big, fast chicane.

The nerves have disappeared and I'm focusing on braking markers, turn-in points, apexes. My head's down, I take no risks and make no mistakes and, before I know it, I'm out of the last corner and looking for my pit-board – a summary of key information held out for me by my team, which I can glance at as I go back down the start-finish straight. I want to see the gap, in seconds, over the rider immediately behind me.

I catch a glimpse as I scream past. It's +0.0.

No way. That can't be! I've made a perfect start and done a great first lap. I've been so quick all weekend – I must have some kind of small margin at least.

One lap later, the gap is reading +1.5. That's more like it. I'm away, determined to start building a lead and control the race from the front.

Then I see red flags – the race has been stopped.

A bike has crashed into a strip of air fencing, puncturing the inflatable barrier. I see it as I ride past turn five and I know we're going to have to wait for a replacement unit, which is going to take a few minutes. I roll back up the pit-lane and into the garage where Pere is saying everything's great, we're in control. I asked him why the gap was +0.0 on the first lap and he says it wasn't, it was +0.9. I must have been looking at my team-mate's pit-board and not my own. It's the first time in the whole weekend all the pit-boards have been held out at the same time, so I need to concentrate on finding mine. I ask Kev for another visor with three tear-offs because there are a lot of bugs out there. I hate having bugs on my visor – I'd be useless at the TT.

Now we have to go out and do a quick-start procedure – a sighting lap, one mechanic on the grid to show me my start position, no tyre warmers. Another quick warm-up lap and more stress trying to find neutral, rolling up for the second start. Another routine nod to Uri and we're waiting for the lights again. I've got the bike held in launch control mode, but now there's another problem – the lights just kind of flicker and then go off again. Yellow flags everywhere. A board is held out of the starter's position above the track: Start Delayed. It's the right call from a safety point-of-view, but this race is fucked up.

I switch off the engine straight away because it's over-heating, and I wait for the mechanics to swarm back out to the grid and put the tyre warmers back on. I take another visor from Kev, because I always use a tear-off on the warm-up lap. Race control puts out a sign saying the race has been reduced to 16 laps. Off we go again – another warm-up lap, another fumble for neutral, but this time I'm worried I might have fried the clutch on the aborted start. Normally, my crew changes the clutch after one practice start. We're about to do our third in this race.

I'm back in my grid position, the start marshal is walking off and the lights come on again, without any problem, and they go out after a similar wait. I get another good start, focus again on my braking marker and turn in for the first corner, only this time I go in pretty equal with my team-mate

Tom, who's starting from pole position. He is virtually on top of me as he tips in, causing me to sit up a bit.

So, this is first contact with the enemy – and that battle plan agreed with Fab duly goes out the window.

Fuck this. Instead of waiting for five laps for the race to settle down, I'm taking control.

I take a slightly wider line than Tom through turn one, pulling the bike back to a really late apex so I can square off the end of the corner and get on the gas hard. I cut across the kerb on the inside of turn two and rocket past Tom so fast on the drag down to turn three.

Don't out-brake yourself. Just hit the apex, pick the bike up quickly for turn four and block him in case he tries to get back round. I'm still in front as I charge down to turn five. Now I can manage the race.

I complete a great first lap, check the pit-board – the right one this time – and it reads +0.4 and the next time around it's +1.1, after a 1m 59.535s lap. It turns out to be the fastest lap of the race and perhaps promises another Pirelli Best Lap moment of TV gold (as long as I don't need another piss).

The gap continues to grow, but on lap four a bug splats right in the middle of my visor, directly in my field of vision. I'm in a dilemma: if I use a tear-off now, I'll only have one left to last the rest of the race. I decide to push on, squinting around what's left of the bug.

Arturo's on my pit-board and he's almost telepathic in knowing what information I need to see. The gap has continued to build, but now it's Marco Melandri directly behind me – he must have passed Tom, unless Tom's had a problem. I start to wonder if Melandri's found some extra speed for the race, but Arturo is instinctively putting the Italian's lap times below his name on my board as well – it's reading +3.5, Melandri, 00.5 (his lap time of 2m 00.5s) and I can see from my dash that I've just done a 2m 00.3s. If I can keep doing that, two- or three-tenths each lap faster than the guy behind me, I can keep pulling away. He's not going to catch me.

This is my mindset – every corner, every sector, every lap – for the rest of the race: check the pit-board and keep going that little bit quicker than Melandri.

I've done so many laps of Brno over the weekend, plus a test here a few weeks ago. I know exactly where to brake, where to turn in, how each corner should feel – it's metronomic, instinctive. But it's the hottest part of the weekend and the front tyre is starting to degrade. As I roll gently off the gas and go into corners with some lean angle, the bars start to rock a little in my hands because the tyre is moving underneath me.

The rubber is so hot that the molecules in the tyre's construction are moving around inside the compound. I'm aware of it as I go through the stadium section, turns five and six especially.

The front tyre is tapping me on the shoulder and saying, 'Hey, this is the limit for today.'

If Melandri doesn't have this problem, if his bike is set up a little differently and putting less stress on the tyre, he's going to catch me. But I see the pit-board again, and the gap is still increasing: +3.8, +4.1, +4.5, +4.7. Just keep doing what you're doing, don't make any mistakes. Suddenly, my pit-board is reading L1, the final lap, I'm +5.1, and only now do I start thinking about actually winning the race.

I'm powering up the hill towards the end of the lap for the last time and the bike wheelies a little before the final chicane, turns 13 and 14.

As I exit the last corner, I catch another wheelie perfectly and cross the line on the back wheel, standing up, nodding to my crew who are crawling all over the pit-wall fence.

They're holding a board that displays a specially-designed logo – 60 victories, Recordman – and that mantra.

Dream. Believe. Achieve.

I hardly take any of it in, because I'm still pulling this insane wheelie that feels so good I carry it the entire length of the straight, almost down to turn one. Then, as I land the front wheel, the pit-board message hits me.

It's my 60th World Superbike victory.

Not bad for a country lad built for motocross.

I roll round turn one, taking it in.

Oh my God! I've got the most Superbike race wins in history. More victories than any other rider since the championship began; one more than the Superbike legend that is Carl Fogarty, whose record stood for almost 20 years. The team's marketing manager, Biel Roda, spoke to me about this moment earlier this morning but I barely took it in. 'Hey,' he said, 'if something happens today, we'll be at turn 11, OK?' I knew what he meant and I just replied 'Cool, OK.'

I do the slow-down lap pretty much on my own, because I had such a big lead at the end of the race. I get to turn 11 quite quickly where Biel is waiting with Ruben Coca, one of the technical guys, and Silvia Sanchez, the team co-ordinator and life and soul of the entire organisation.

It's so cool to see them all there, and they've got a special T-shirt and flag prepared for me. As I pull on the T-shirt, I start to realise I've made some history.

How did I get here? It's been one hell of a ride …

CHAPTER 2

IN THE BLOOD

MOTORCYCLE RACING IS in my blood: my grandad sponsored a lot of great Northern Irish riders like Joey Dunlop, and my dad Johnny was an Irish Road Racing Champion.

I very nearly didn't come along at all though. Dad and my mum Claire hadn't been going out long when, during a race at Brands Hatch, Dad collided with another rider. It was at Paddock Hill Bend in the days before there was any run-off and he smashed into the barrier. He was on life support at Queen Mary's Hospital, London, for over a week after puncturing a lung and fracturing six ribs. In an operation to stop internal bleeding he lost a kidney. Mum didn't know if he was going to make it. Almost as soon as he woke up, he proposed.

They were married a year later and soon enough I was on the way. Even in the womb I was listening to the roar of engines and the vibes and talk of paddock life. When I first drew breath at 4.20pm on Monday, 2 February 1987 at the Waveney Hospital, Ballymena, the midwife was crazy about bikes and spent most of the labour gabbing away about them to Dad. I was taken home to our rented house in Starbog Road, Kilwaughter – a little village near Larne in

County Antrim – and I was christened at the First Lane Presbyterian Church by Rev. Lambert McAdoo, who happened to be another massive bike fan.

When I got colic the only thing that would keep me quiet was being strapped into a bouncy chair in the back of the car and being driven around for hours on end. This lasted until they fitted a proper car seat, which I hated so much I'd climb out as soon as Mum started driving. One day, I spotted a motorcyclist wearing a familiar-looking white Arai helmet and I was screaming 'Daddy! Daddy!' at him. The police wore Arai helmets in those days; that particular copper gave me a gentle talking to about staying in my seat.

My favourite TV shows were *Fireman Sam*, *Thomas the Tank Engine* and the motorcycle racing. I'd sit on the arm of the sofa wearing Dad's helmet, leaning into the corners with the guys on the screen. Later, I organised my own bicycle races around the house, with Mum recording my lap times. I would commentate, then do my own post-race interviews, asking the questions and answering in an American accent like my early heroes, Kevin Schwantz and Jeremy McGrath. When I started nursery school in Ballyclare, there was a sponsored cycle ride that, of course, wasn't supposed to be a race. But I made sure I finished first and took my first chequered flag.

Dad had started racing motocross when he was about 14, but 'Granda' John said it was 'dirty and mucky' so he switched to short circuit and road racing later and did pretty well. He won Irish and Ulster championships and the famous Ulster Grand Prix, always his favourite event. He never finished higher than second at the North West 200, but he did win the 1989 Lightweight TT on the Isle of Man on a 250cc Yamaha. To even compete in a TT race is something – to win one is something else.

Now, you may have noticed a little name pattern emerging: although my dad is called Johnny, he was christened John Rea, as was Granda, and there were three generations of John Rea before that. I was the first grandson in the line, so I was destined to become the sixth consecutive John Rea. My parents called me Jonathan, but that doesn't stop me being called John and Johnny.

It was Granda who started the whole racing thing in the family. He had the nickname 'Stormy' because when he lost his temper you could hear him from miles away. He and his three brothers got into racing because they lived near the old Ulster Grand Prix course at Clady. Granda never raced himself but loved going down to watch and before long the brothers started backing road racers. Then someone told him about this young kid from Ballymoney, Joey Dunlop, who was fast but didn't have any bikes. Granda sponsored Joey in his early road racing days with that famous understated 'Rea Racing' logo on the side of his fairings. Joey went on to become one of Northern Ireland's greatest racing heroes, winning a record 26 races at the Isle of Man TT and five Formula TT World Championships. A few years ago, he was voted Northern Ireland's greatest ever sports star by *Belfast Telegraph* readers.

I have nothing but happy memories of Granda. Mostly involving apples. I remember going up to his place and chatting about bikes, crunching on apples. He used to say, 'You know, you're just like your dad.' I was still young and wasn't sure what he meant. But he said it a lot: 'You're just like your dad and you'll be a fine wee racer. You'll be a world champion, so you will.'

Mum's mother, 'Nanna', was a nurse and her father a contractor. Nanna is an amazingly strong and traditional Northern Irish lady and lived just off the North West 200 course when I was young. Being very religious, Sundays have always been a day of rest for her. So, my chosen career, which involved going to work on a Sunday, was a huge 'tut-tut' back in the day and I felt quite guilty about upsetting her.

Nanna eventually got used to the idea of me racing and I've watched her go full circle and become my number one fan. She's much more relaxed about watching me go to work on a Sunday now.

I've had some of the most sincere but funniest post-race telephone calls with Nanna, especially during my days riding with Honda. She texts before and after every race and tells me she's been asking God to keep me safe. I love getting her messages, but it would be impossible to reply to them all, so, once in a while, I'll call her to make up for the radio silence. One time, I rang after a race in 2012 when I had a bit of time at the airport. It was a period when we were really struggling with the Honda and she'd been listening to the Eurosport race commentary of Jack Burnicle and James Whitham. She's normally totally calm, but she sounded pretty mad and said they'd been talking about how the

Honda was at the end of the line and how I was having to override it. She took it all as gospel and said, 'Jonathan, it's terrible they're making you ride that bike. They're saying that you're always close to making a mistake and that it's difficult for you to realise your potential.'

I said, 'Nanna, it is what it is – the team are doing the best they can. It's not their fault but the base level of the Honda is just not competitive enough.'

'Well, it's not fair,' she said, 'they say you're always riding on a knife edge.'

I told her that the bike was mass produced at the factory in Japan and that there wasn't much we could do about it. She said, 'So give me the number of the people over there, I want to call them and tell them it's not fair they're making you ride that bike.'

I couldn't help laughing down the phone with her, but she was deadly serious. I promised that I would have a word with the Japanese engineers and get them to try to make a better bike.

Mum was very good at sport when she was young and really competitive. She played hockey for Randalstown Ladies, one of Northern Ireland's top women's teams, and did athletics to county level, but she hurt her back in a long-jump competition, aged 16, and had to give it all up.

Living close to the North West 200 course meant she saw her first race there when she was about 13. Unfortunately, she witnessed the crash in which Tom Herron was killed. He was one of Ireland's highest-profile racers and had just started his Grand Prix career as a team-mate to Barry

Sheene. Understandably, she never really enjoyed our time at the North West 200 after that but was apparently more relaxed watching my dad race at the Isle of Man TT where she could monitor his progress around the course from a massive board at the main grandstand.

My very first holiday, at the age of three months, was going with Mum to see Dad in that North West 200, where we had a caravan in the paddock. Our summer half-term holiday was often a week on the Isle of Man where Dad was racing at the TT. Mum tells me that from a very young age I would just stand at the fence and not move for hours. I could recite the race numbers of all the riders as well, and it's kind of spooky that my son Jake did exactly the same with World Superbike riders from about the same age.

When I was a bit older, I just used to love getting in the way in the paddock and was always really happy to feel part of the team when Dad gave me little jobs like cleaning wheels or polishing the bikes.

Mum tells this story about one weekend when I was about three-and-a-half and we all went down south to a place called Loughshinny near Dublin to watch Dad race. He had quite a bad crash and as he lay in the road another bike had come along and whacked him properly in the nuts. I can't imagine the pain he must have been in, and although we can laugh about it now, he would have been in agony. He spent a couple of weeks in hospital and by the time he'd recovered his sense of humour he was telling anyone who'd listen that he was the only white man in the world with a black dick and took great pleasure showing his battle scars to his mates who went to visit.

Despite Mum's bad memories of that episode, and the North West and the Brands Hatch crashes, she supported Dad's career on top of being mum to four of us kids: me the eldest, Richard, Kristofer (who we jokingly call the Mistake!) and Chloe.

Richard turned out to be a pretty good kid brother, by which I mean his arrival in November 1989 was probably one of the best things to happen in my early life. He and I spent a lot of years having fun and riding bikes together and he has turned out to be one of the nicest, most genuine blokes I've ever known. He's a real gentle giant and has become a very important influence in my life. The arrival of Kristofer and Chloe made us a much bigger family unit and those years of expansion must have been a pretty chaotic time for my parents.

Mum was never any kind of pushover, but if Dad came home and she told him that we'd not done something or we'd been naughty, he would shout a bit and whatever it was that we hadn't done got sorted pretty quickly. You could say I had a fairly strict upbringing, and although I don't remember actually being hit with anything, the threat of getting a bit of a whack if we were naughty was never far away.

I totally respected my parents while I was growing up and I still do. They really helped my growing love of motorcycles too. Dad's TT win in 1989 came, of course, with a bit of prize money and he bought me the best Christmas present I could imagine: an Italjet 50, a tiny little motocross-style bike. I was just short of my third birthday.

Unfortunately, Santa's amazing generosity hadn't stretched to a helmet, or any gloves or boots; but that wasn't going to stop me riding on that cold Christmas Day. Dad probably instantly regretted it. He must have frozen his nuts off watching me ride up and down all day outside in the cold. I knew how to twist the throttle, because Dad had shown me when he used to sit me on his race bikes from the minute I could hold myself up. But he had to explain what the brakes were all about. The problem was I still couldn't get the bike stopped because my hands were too small for my fingers to reach the brake lever, so Dad had to run alongside to make sure I didn't ride into a fence or the side of the house. I just rode and rode all day until the bike ran out of fuel. Not surprisingly, I had my first crash that day, but it didn't put me off – I was straight back on it, because I loved it and never wanted to get off.

Looking back at my early life, you can see a lot of me as a professional racer coming together. I used to throw a complete fit if we were ever late for Ballynure Primary and Mum had to be waiting outside as soon as I came out in the afternoon. An early love of routine and following a schedule, I guess, which helps for busy race weekends today. I also got an early taste of hospitals, now an occupational hazard, when I had suspected meningitis and was kept isolated on a drip for about five days.

I got in plenty of training, too. The house in Kilwaughter was, for me, the ultimate kid's playground. We had a reasonably sized garden and the land backed onto the Kilwaughter House Hotel, which, in the mid-1990s, was one of the biggest rave venues in Northern Ireland. We had a pretty good relationship with the hotel management and, while we were OK about the ravers trampling all over the place every weekend, they were quite relaxed about me using the hotel grounds to practise riding whenever I could. The house also backed onto a limestone quarry and chemical works, which was just like an extension of the playground for me and Richard and my schoolfriend Philip McCammond on our BMX bikes.

Philip is an absolute legend, a lifelong friend, and he introduced me to this other playground down the road, which happened to be his parents' farm. Our two families were inseparable. Lorraine, Philip's mother, was like my second mum and Richard also became best friends with Michael, Philip's younger brother. With them living on a farm, it made riding motorcycles on private property much easier as well.

One night, when Dad and Philip's dad Gary were working on the bikes at our house in Kilwaughter, me, Philip and his bigger brother Christopher ventured out of the garage and wandered up among the trees of the hotel where we saw a couple basically dry humping the life out of each other. We started laughing, but it got less funny when the two of them suddenly broke off, especially when we saw the expression on the fella's face. They chased us down through the woods and Christopher and I managed to get back to the garage, but Philip wasn't so quick and they caught him by the scruff of the neck.

It was the first time I'd seen Dad properly rear up and he charged out of the garage with this big lump hammer, shouting, 'If you don't let him go, I'm going to hammer you!' The fella let go pretty quickly and started running very fast in the opposite direction.

There were some stables at the hotel, which belonged to my dad's Uncle Noel, and I remember Richard got a horse once when he was drifting in and out of bikes. He was a funny old nag with a glass eye that we called Flash. Much to Mum's horror, Richard, Philip and I used to climb aboard Flash and ride him, without any training or technique, just to see how fast we could go and how high we could get him to jump.

Once, probably after the parents had all had a few drinks, it was suggested we should build a proper motocross track on some rough ground in one of the fields on the farm. So, our dads got a local guy with a JCB to come in and we gave him a good idea of what we wanted. He put together a really cool track for us, with double jumps and tabletops and everything you'd want for a little motocross track.

When I wasn't riding I was at home watching motocross videos. I would devour anything: Supercross re-runs, training videos, Grand Prix races, any kind of racing. I would watch them over and over on repeat, studying them in as much detail as I could, looking at race starts, the different techniques of individual riders, how they rode inside or outside corners, through ruts, how they took jumps and whoops.

Apart from motocross, I remember watching Kevin Schwantz in 1993 and 1994 doing his thing in 500cc GPs because my dad was always a fan of his. I used to make tracks out of anything that happened to be lying around to race my little model of his Pepsi Suzuki.

As soon as I climbed on that little Italjet, I knew I never really wanted to be anywhere else. But while little kids grow, motorcycles don't, so it wasn't too long before I was riding a Yamaha PW50, which was as iconic back then as it is today. I remember mine vividly – white plastics with a bright red seat and displaying race number 17. I spent day after day riding the bike around the garden at home and at the McCammonds' farm.

I was desperate to start racing myself. It happened that the final round of the 1993 British Youth Motocross Championship was coming to Ireland's famous track at Desertmartin, a tiny village in County Londonderry not far from Cookstown. The track is one of the best in the world and has hosted many world and British championship races.

We applied for a wildcard for the 50cc race – a one-off entry rather than entering for a whole championship. A low-profile junior club meeting would have been a fine first race but, no, we were jumping straight in at the deep end. To my six-year-old eyes, everything in this paddock was huge. It was full of swanky 30ft motorhomes and big sponsored teams from the national series. And there was us in our little white van and a PW50.

The 50cc class at that time featured a mix of standard bikes like my PW50 and tuned machines that were more like a real race bike with a proper motocross chassis – bikes like LEMs and Malagutis, which were much better and faster. I lined up at the start on my little standard bike with what felt like the pressure of the world on my shoulders because I wanted to do so well.

I'd been riding for two or three years by then, with coaching and encouragement from Dad, so I was comfortable on the bike. I'd been watching Dad racing and often winning for as long as I could remember. I was always aware of his nerves in the build-up to a race; he'd smoke a bit more and go into himself. Suddenly, this was me racing – my dad was watching me, and I could sense he was nervous as well. I knew it was a really important moment: there was Granda's prediction to fulfil. I wasn't scared though; I just knew I had to do a good job.

I memorised all the names and race numbers I was lining up against, even though I'd never met them. I was surrounded by about 30 noisy little two-stroke bikes with riders blipping throttles and creating this huge noise of anticipation and clouds of blue smoke that just seemed to hang in the air. Lining up at the gate, I was sure I was going to get smoked by all these bigger kids on their impressive bikes, but Dad was telling me not to worry: they could only score points in their modified class, while I would be competing in the separate class for standard bikes like my PW50. It was like the independent class we have today in World Superbikes and MotoGP, a race within a race.

In some ways, there's not much difference between me lining up then and now. Nervous, but focused and a little detached – like the lights are on but no-one's in. I was trying just to concentrate on doing my best, like my dad had told me. I sat and waited quietly.

Motocross racers start in one straight line held by metal gates which all drop together when the starter is ready. I just stared at this gate, waiting for it to fall so we could get going.

Suddenly, there was this howl of 30 throttles being snapped open to maximum revs and we all took off. This was it, I was racing and heading for the first turn, trying not to hit any of the other riders but it was all pretty chaotic. I got through the first few turns and slotted into some kind of rhythm.

On the third lap, I rode through a puddle and got water in the electrics. The little temperamental PW just stopped. I sat in the middle of that big puddle in floods of tears. Someone had to come and get me off the track before the other riders came round again. Afterwards, Mum and Dad told me everything was OK but, for a long time, it wasn't.

When the tears had dried and I'd calmed down a bit, I couldn't wait to have another go.

CHAPTER 3

MOTOCROSS

I WAS STILL only six when Granda died, aged just 67. The night before the funeral, his open coffin was in the house and, even though the kids weren't encouraged to go in, I wanted to see him. He didn't look any different to me; he just looked peaceful. The next day there were a lot of tears flowing from my dad and his family; it was the first time I saw adults cry, but maybe it was because my grandfather had looked so normal the night before that I just carried on playing with my friends.

I didn't appreciate it at the time, but Granda had a high profile in Irish racing and made a big impact with his sponsorship. Even now, Irish racing fans from the 1980s or 90s are always happy to tell me what a grand fella my grandfather was. He's certainly a massive part of what made me a racer, which really started to get going that year.

After that first wildcard ride at Desertmartin, we managed a few more open track sessions so I could study puddle-avoidance techniques. The bug had bitten, I was desperate to race again, so it was decided that in 1994 we would give it a proper go and we prepared to head off on the most incredible adventure.

I was lucky enough to get one of those trick modified 50cc bikes I'd seen – a Malaguti Grizzly, a genuinely fast little bike. We raced all over Ireland, in the north on Saturdays and the south on Sundays. I loved every minute of the next few years on the Malaguti and later on a 60cc Kawasaki. I was living this exciting sporting life with my family every weekend, playing with my brother, Richard, and my best friend Philip, who were also racing – just like we did on the farm and in Kilwaughter. I got a massive thrill out of the racing, running through things with Dad, checking out the track and the lines other racers used. Riding the bike itself was just an enormous buzz, especially if I did well in the races. Back then, after a race, win or lose, I was able to muck about with my mates and spend time in the little close-knit family unit that we had.

Once, Richard was supposed to be lining up for a race but was nowhere to be seen. We found him sitting under the awning about to get stuck into a big cheeseburger. Dad said, 'What do you think you're doing? They're all lined up ready to go!' Richard replied through a mouthful of burger, 'Could you ask them to hang on, Dad?' Dad's face said that he wasn't about to do that, but he always understood Richard's attitude to racing was a little different to mine. He said, 'Well, you'll just have to miss the race then.' He finished his burger.

Richard was never that fast on a motocross bike, God love him. He was riding ahead of me at an open practice day at a new track in southern Ireland when I launched this huge double jump and saw him riding up the other side where I was planning to land. I hit the end of his handlebar and broke his wrist then came down and broke my collarbone. Mum came running over and put her foot in a rabbit hole and twisted her ankle.

So, all three of us were sitting in an ambulance on our way to A&E and the whole way Richard is asking the paramedics, 'Do you know if the hospital food's any good?' – not seeming to care that his wrist was in bits. Mum said, 'Shut up, Richard! This is not the time to be worrying about food!' I was more concerned about missing any races because of my collarbone, but that's where we differ, Richard and me – we're cut from slightly different cloth! He was happy enough with a takeaway Chinese we had when we finally got home, but we were all in a hell of a state sitting round the family table eating that meal.

Normal injuries could get complicated, too. One time I was in hospital and one of the nurses noticed I was covered in roost marks across my upper arms and chest, which often happens when riders in front of you kick up clumps of mud and stones with their rear tyres. The medical staff wouldn't let my parents into the ward to see me – they were more concerned with whether they should be calling social services.

At the end of the first season, Mum took me and Richard to a meeting where I won four races. I was so excited but as soon as I'd finished, Mum packed us all into the van and drove like crazy to get us to Bishopscourt where Dad was racing in a popular end-of-season meeting. We watched from a grass bank, me still in my bright pink motocross gear and super-excited to tell Dad about my wins. He listened then said, 'I only managed a seventh. It's probably time I hung up my leathers.' So that was it, 1994 was his final year of racing. I wasn't complaining too much though; it meant I got to go motocrossing a lot more.

Over those years, I did better and better and ended up with another wildcard in the final round of the British championship at Desertmartin in 1996. I had a much better race than in my first puddle-bound outing so we decided that for 1997, when I was 10, we'd tackle the full British championship. Dad saw that there was this strong family atmosphere and social thing going on and eventually he sold the idea to Mum.

It was a massively big deal for us – me, my dad and his mate Sandy travelling the length and breadth of the UK for me to race bikes. I particularly remember the first round, at a circuit in Cheshire called Cheddleton, which had a railway track running through it at the bottom of a hill. I was feeling quite confident on my Kawasaki KX60 – the engine was strong and the suspension was great after we'd done lots of testing with my dad. But it looked completely standard, right down to the manufacturer's stickers, and we were running a standard exhaust. I could see all these trick bikes with exotic aftermarket parts and sponsor stickers and began to feel very intimidated again. But Dad would always tell me, 'Don't worry about how the bike looks, it's how it goes that matters.' He was right: maybe the competition back in Ireland had been tougher than I thought because I won those first races. And on day two, most of my rivals rocked up with standard exhausts back on their bikes.

I could fill a separate book with every race of my moto-cross career and every feeling I had in the build-up, on the start line and at the end – I can remember every single one.

There were few better than the end of the 1997 British championship. At a week-long festival before the final weekend at Desertmartin, I had a couple of huge crashes landing on a double jump that followed a big tabletop. Twice I picked my rut too late and ended up cross rutting – when your front wheel goes into one rut and your rear is in another – and twice I crashed. I became really anxious and scared to do the double jump again over the weekend.

Dad could see my confidence was completely gone and gave a senior rider called Adam Lyons a few quid to do a track walk with me. He helped me cope by talking me through exactly how to deal with the jumps with those deep ruts. When the first race came I had a great start, leading through the first few corners to the big tabletop. The 60cc bikes couldn't quite clear the flat part like bigger, more powerful bikes, so I landed on it and bounced down the other side towards the jump where I'd had those huge crashes a couple of days before. When you're ahead with a clear track in front of you, it's the best opportunity to make time on your rivals, so I picked the rut I was aiming for as soon I found the down slope of the tabletop and nailed it first time. From that point my confidence was back, I built a massive lead and ended up winning all four races that weekend to become British champion.

There were so many special moments that year. In the build-up, I was interviewed by Stephen Watson, the BBC's sports presenter and a big motorcycling fan. He had asked me then about my future plans and I told him to watch out for the Rea name.

I also won the Irish and Ulster Motocross Championships back home. British Prime Minister Tony Blair even wrote to congratulate me!

Dad did a great job of keeping my feet on the ground though. I wanted the world and couldn't wait for it to come to me. I remember later being desperate for some white Tech 7 Alpinestar boots and eventually Mum went against Dad's wishes and bought me a pair, but he wasn't happy. He believed you had to strive and wait for the good things in life. Mum was the same, but I could manipulate her a bit better.

Mum is a very loving, nurturing character. She can get a bit stressed sometimes and have very strong opinions but will often back them up if she's challenged on them. She was the glue that held the whole family together both at home and while we were on the schoolboy motocross adventure.

While Dad was sympathetic as I sat in that puddle at Desertmartin, he never showed much emotion. He is a quiet, humble man who likes to just watch from a distance, often puffing away on a cigarette.

In the final race of my second year in the modified 50cc class, I got pipped to the championship by my good friend Martin Barr and bawled my head off. He was very calm and said, 'Look, you're going to get beaten sometimes and you'll just have to accept it.'

At the time that just pissed me off even more! But now I feel I'm a really well-rounded rider and I have my dad to thank for that. I'm always trying to make my sons see that a pair of white Tech 7 Alpinestars is something you have to long for. But Alpinestars are one of my biggest and most loyal sponsors, so my four-year-old son Jake's already got a pair. I had to wait until I was 14.

I was always aware I had a responsibility to do my bit and, because I was a terrible mechanic, I was happy to wash the bikes down and polish everything until it shone. Dad often said to me, 'While things might not look perfect and you might not be wearing the latest gear, your bikes will always be good.' As usual he was right – thanks to him my bikes never missed a beat and never broke down.

He must have spent thousands of hours fettling the bikes and driving thousands of miles for me to go racing. He would never put me down, but I knew if we were travelling in silence I hadn't done a great job. He never went over the top when I won either; he's not the kind to spray the champagne.

I learned so much in those years just by racing and trying to get better: How to apply the throttle to get maximum traction out of the corners on dirt; how to use the front and rear brakes in combination – applying and releasing to create a balance and prevent the bike pitching back and forth too much. I worked out how to release the clutch lever to make gear changes as smoothly as possible. And I learned how to plan a race. Those 15-minute-plus races were incredibly physical, absorbing bumps and landings from jumps, muscling the bike into and out of corners. I found any way I could to make the races less physical, by taking different, smoother lines or adjusting my body position to make riding less tiring.

When you're riding bar-to-bar with 40 other riders going down to the first corner, you develop this balance of aggression and caution, a kind of sixth sense of what the other riders are going to do. After years of those, launching off the start line of a World Superbike race with three riders on each row of the grid is honestly not that daunting.

Motocross is so raw and is still my first love. We can't even go to a private World Superbike test now without two 40ft trucks, plus the hospitality unit to water and feed around 40 staff. But when I'm at home I can put my motocross bike in the back of my van and go and meet my friends at the track and have a great day riding, having fun. I really love that, but I think if motocross was my job the enjoyment might be different.

I always arrange a motocross camp before each World Superbike season. I put myself through race simulations of about the same time length as a World Superbike race – around 35 minutes – to switch my brain and my muscles on again after a few weeks off the bike. In track racing, the speeds are a lot faster but the environment is extremely controlled. In motocross, the track is always changing and you have to be so alert to all those variations.

My annual camps remind me of my early motocross years, which were one long fantastic adventure. Mum and Dad bought a bigger motorhome and we had what we called the 'coffin bed' above the workshop which I shared with Richard, and the two of us had Chloe, a wee baby at the time, in between us. We'd often get a late ferry back on the Sunday night and my parents would leave us asleep in the motorhome and wake us on the Monday morning for school.

But if the racing was going from strength to strength, school definitely wasn't.

Mum and Dad had said that if I wanted to carry on with motocross, I'd have to pass the 11-plus. I did, but I ended up the only kid from Ballynure to go to my senior school, Larne Grammar – no Philip, no anyone. I knew from the first time I got on the bus just outside the house that I wasn't going to be happy. I struggled from the first day and found it difficult to make friends.

I want to say now that Larne Grammar was a fantastic educational institution. My business studies teacher, Miss Herron, my Spanish teacher, Miss Beggs, and my technology teacher, Mr Lee, are amazing people. But I found it pretty tough. In my first three years there, I really felt what it's like to be bullied. And it's not a nice feeling at all.

You probably know about the religious divide in Northern Ireland and how dramatically it has affected people's lives over the years, especially during the Troubles in the 1970s, 80s and 90s. The Good Friday Agreement, which brought about a permanent peace in the province, was signed in 1998, just a few months before I went to Larne Grammar, a mixed school taking children from Protestant and Catholic families.

My naïve country upbringing hadn't prepared me for life in a school where, to some kids, religion was something to hang on to. The guy who was bullying me was a Catholic, which I couldn't have given two shits about because I had as many Catholic friends as Protestant in my motocross world. But where it gets bat-shit crazy is how it all started – with a Kevin Schwantz pencil case done out in his famous Pepsi colours. You know the Pepsi colours: red, white and blue. Yep, the same as the Union flag. And this, I kid you not, is what kicked it off in school.

My friend Martin Barr lived on a housing estate just outside Ballyclare and the kerbstones there were painted red, white and blue – not unlike the rumble strips at the Assen TT Circuit – obviously for religious and loyalist reasons. I didn't get that at all though and asked if there was a racetrack there. Remember, they race on the roads in Ireland, so it wasn't such a daft question! But, along with my deeply offensive Pepsi pencil case, that was great ammunition for me to be tormented with.

In those days, I'd heard stories of the youth wings of paramilitary groups, but I knew absolutely nothing about how they worked. Thankfully I never found out, but I was often threatened quite menacingly with the possibility of getting jumped or stabbed by some of these guys on my way to or from school.

The whole experience and the relentless and scary nature of it definitely affected my confidence, especially with other kids at school. I just tried to keep my head down and maintain as low a profile as possible. God love Mum, though, she was in the headmaster's office more than enough times because of this problem.

It all came to a head at the end of Year 10 – I would have been about 14 – when we were all lined up to go into the sports hall to do a Key Stage 3 test. Something was said to me by this same bully and for some reason my fuse just blew. I'm not proud of that moment when I was punching him so hard I started crying myself. Violence should never be a way to settle any dispute. But afterwards the bullying stopped and I'm happy to report I was never stabbed on the way home. The last two years became kind of bearable and while the kid and I did not become lifelong best buddies, we got along.

For 2002, Dad put in a massive effort to get a bike good enough for what turned out to be my final 125cc schoolboy season. Right the way through the schoolboy motocross ranks I was always very competitive and won a lot of championships in Ireland, but when we competed in England I always seemed to have an issue in my final year of any particular class, when I should have been most likely to win. There would often be an injury to recover from, or simply faster rivals to deal with.

So, Dad took a Honda CR125R that was already pretty sorted with better suspension and he spent a fortune making it race-ready. Then, just two weeks before the start of the season, our garage got broken into and my bike, my tyre allocation, generators, my brother's quad bike, everything, was stolen by some lowlife.

They had known what they were going in for. The police were getting nowhere, so we started asking around the local area about who might have been responsible. We never quite got to the bottom of it, but we got a pretty good idea. Dad's questions led him, he said, to meet people in some of the scariest pubs he'd ever been to. We had never had any association with those organised crime groups or paramilitary organisations in Northern Ireland, but eventually he got a call from someone whose voice he didn't recognise but who said that he and Dad knew of each other. The mystery caller told Dad he was getting close to our stuff but that, if he knew what was good for him, he'd drop the trail and forget all about it.

We packed our bags pretty quickly after that and moved permanently about five miles further into the countryside, right on the edge of a forest called Ballyboley.

Along with my bike and my realistic hopes for the season, we had to say goodbye to the adventure playground that was Kilwaughter. I'm not saying Dad stopped enjoying racing there and then, but it put a dampener on the whole motocross adventure, I think, for both of us.

I had to start the season borrowing Philip's KTM SX125. It was a horrible bike and never felt right or like it was mine, so that 2002 season was certainly lacking something, and although I was always competitive I never got to win another British schoolboy championship.

By then, I knew I didn't want to continue with A levels or go to university after I left school the next summer, and Mum and Dad made it clear I was never going to be allowed to lie around at home trying to be a professional motocross rider. My parents had always seemed to find a way to finance the racing and Mum was always very good at putting sponsorship proposals together. But they had been funding this adventure for the best part of ten years and now I was going to have to go to work, to earn money and treat motorbikes as a hobby and nothing else.

I was also aware I had two brothers and a sister, and it wasn't fair that my parents had spent so much time and energy allowing me to follow my dreams. Dad had taken over Granda's transport business, which is still going strong now, and that needed more of his attention. It was getting to the point that my ambition was in one place and reality was in another.

I'd grown up and raced in the early motocross days with the Laverty brothers, who made the transition to road racing with some success and appeared to live this glamorous life as professional racers. I wanted some of that for myself and, seeing them ride, I was sure I could do the same. I was also a bit envious of some of my rivals who were starting to train in the USA during the winter, some of them even home-schooled because their parents were so loaded and committed.

I knew it was going to be tough to earn money from racing, but I had to give it a go. I began flirting with the idea of trying to scrape together enough personal sponsorship to buy a ride in 2003 with a bigger, manufacturer-supported team from the UK, a process where I would pay for a ride by covering the costs of the bike or the tyre budget or, in some cases, much more.

I met a guy called Stevie Mills, who has become a great friend, and he helped me look for a professional seat.

Another friend, Gareth Crichton, picked up on more of the spannering as Dad started to roll off the throttle a bit during that 2002 season, and we had a lot of discussions about where it was all heading. I was at a crossroads. A few of my dad's racing friends offered me bikes to go pure road racing, like at the Isle of Man TT, but that wasn't for me. I also had an opportunity through Dad's link with Joe Millar, a great friend of Granda and high-profile sponsor, to get hold of a 125cc Honda race bike that we could run ourselves. But that was short-circuit racing and that seemed a huge leap considering I'd never ridden on tarmac.

It was around this time that Arenacross became popular in the UK. Arenacross was the equivalent of Supercross in the USA, where a compact motocross track is built with around 5,000 tonnes of earth shipped into an indoor arena.

I rode in one event for a guy called Darren Wilson at the Odyssey Arena, Belfast. Darren got hold of an ex-factory GP bike, Stevie hooked me up with all the gear and Mum took me for a bit of practice without Dad knowing. I remember Darren pushing the bike up to the start in the dark with all the music blaring out, the flashing lights and the announcer hyping everybody up on the PA. My name was called, and 8,000 people were cheering. My heart rate was probably higher than it's ever been, and I got awfully bad arm-pump during the races but managed to split 1–2 finishes with Shaun Simpson, who's still a GP rider now. I threw my goggles into the crowd at the end of the race I won – it felt like proper rock star stuff!

I think it opened a few people's eyes to what I could do and gave me a little taste of the life of a Supercross rider in the USA where, like everything else, the show, the spectacle, the size of the arena and crowds are ten times the size. I would have jumped at any opportunity to go and do it in the USA, but there was no real evidence of any motocross rider from the UK making it big in Supercross.

After the buzz died down, I could see the reality of my situation. My options about what to do the following year were kind of drying up.

CHAPTER 4

RED BULL ROOKIE

AT THE END of the 2002 season, Gareth Crichton told me about this advert he'd seen in *Motor Cycle News*, the weekly industry newspaper. It was for a kind of audition for a ride with a team in a short-circuit racing programme run by Red Bull and Honda. It was called the Red Bull Rookies and Gareth had already spoken to Dad about it in detail. They thought it would be a good idea to go for it, especially because opportunities in motocross were really drying up, along with Dad's ability to finance it.

The grab headline said, 'Deal worth £70,000', which kind of got my attention, but none of it was going to the rider; it would cover the cost of a bike, spares, tyres, a mechanic, pretty much everything to do a season's racing in the British 125cc Championship except travelling expenses. We thought. 'Wow! This is our *X Factor* – let's try and do this!'

The Red Bull Rookies already had two riders – Midge Smart and Guy Farbrother, who was sadly killed in a road crash just after the start of the following season. They wanted a third rider, aged 14 to 17, with bike experience, and I had to provide a CV and write 40 words on why I should be picked. I wrote mine in bullet points like 'hard-working … willing to learn … enjoys working with others … Ulster, Irish and British Motocross champion … Arenacross race winner … wants to be world champion'.

It must have worked. Of hundreds who responded, I made the first cut of 20. I couldn't believe it. I was still in two minds at that stage, keeping my eyes and ears open for any possible options to continue with motocross, but I couldn't help getting a bit excited about being shortlisted. In his practical way, Dad reminded me there was a way to go yet.

We were invited to Rockingham Motor Speedway in Northamptonshire for a selection day to whittle those 20 down to five. There was only one problem: I'd never ridden a road bike in my life.

This was when Dad's experience and contacts list came in handy. He made some calls, one to an old TT rival and former Grand Prix rider, Ron Haslam. A couple of weeks later, we were on our way to a race school Ron still runs at Donington Park, to ride a Honda CB500 naked road bike. I was wearing my dad's old leathers about five sizes too big, boots a size too small and gloves which fitted. Thanks to Wendy Hearn, an old contact of Dad's who worked for Arai, I also had a shiny new helmet. I've worn Arai ever since.

I'd never been to any kind of racing activity with a kitbag on an airplane before, it was always me and Dad out of the back of the van. But on this trip, me and Dad rocked up at East Midlands airport and stayed in the Holiday Inn Express there – it all felt quite professional. Ron and his wife Ann came to pick us up and take us to a briefing, because it was my first track session. Ron was a bit of a British racing legend and GP hero from the 1970s and 80s, so I felt very special being taken under his wing for some one-to-one coaching sessions.

Ron looked after me really well, and maybe there was a bit of special treatment through knowing my dad. After a few laps, he said, 'You need to be a lot less rigid on the bike. Forget your upright motocross riding style. Move your inside bum cheek off the seat and lean into the corner with the bike.' For ten years, I'd been kind of pushing the bike down into corners and almost pivoting from the middle of the seat, so I told him how alien it felt. But he was calm and reassuring and said, 'Don't worry, it's normal for circuit rookies to be a bit scared at first of leaning your body so much into corners.'

In the middle of the day, Ron said, 'Come on, I'll give you an idea of what I mean.' He got me on the pillion seat of one of the school's Honda Fireblades and took me around for a few laps. He showed me what he meant about moving around on the bike and did a one-handed wheelie down the start-finish straight with me on the back.

I also remember the best piece of advice Dad gave me – which was to make sure to do all your braking in a straight line because, as you release the brake and lean the bike into the corner, the contact patch of the tyre changes. Even now, I still use a fine balance of different braking techniques, trying to get it right for each corner.

When you're riding on tarmac, pretty much all your braking is done with the front brake, whereas in motocross you don't use the front so much and, if anything, the rear is more dominant. The thrill of the higher speeds was just amazing.

At the end of the day, Ron told me he thought I had loads of potential and to keep working at it. 'Hang off the bike more,' he said, 'and you'll be fine at the Rockingham test day.'

I was anxious all the same; I realised I was getting desperate to be picked. This was a really big deal – the kind of opportunity that wasn't going to come my way with motocross.

When we got to Rockingham, it was the worst possible day to have to ride for your future career. It was damp and drizzly and the track surface started out patchy. Tyre choice was an absolute nightmare – at least it would have been if we'd actually had a choice! We had borrowed an old 125 from another contact of Dad's, Alan Patterson, a GP rider back in the early 1990s. We had a set of slicks on the bike and a set of wets for extreme rainy conditions, both of which were pretty old and ropey.

I think the organisers took it all into account and knew that not everything we brought was going to be perfect even though, like in our motocross days, everything was clean and tidy and well presented. They came and had some chats during the day about my racing experience, ambitions and targets. I answered as politely as possible and tried to sound knowledgeable. We didn't really have much of a clue about the carburation, which is vitally important on a 125, or suspension, and whether that had been set up for me or, more specifically, my weight, so we just put the tyre warmers on the bike.

Of the 20 guys at the test, I was the only complete rookie – the others had done at least a season of road racing at club or British championship level. I went out on slicks but, because it was damp, I took it quite steady in the first session.

To my great surprise, I was passing loads of other riders.

My confidence was growing as I remembered my day with Ron Haslam and all the advice he'd given me. I was realising it was working, that hanging off the bike and leaning into the corners allowed you go round the corners faster. And, as anyone who rides a bike will know, the faster you can go round a corner, the bigger the buzz.

I was probably still quite stiff on the bike, but all the levers and pedals were in the same place as on a motocross bike so it was a question of adjusting my balance on the little 125, tucking in behind the screen on the straights and sticking my knee out in the corners instead of extending a leg.

The track was beginning to dry out and I was building speed lap by lap as the dry line got bigger and wider, cutting my lap times not just by tenths of a second but by seconds and seconds. I was passing other riders, amazing myself at how natural everything felt and how quickly I was able to get into a rhythm, moving around on the bike like Ron had told me, using the brakes like my dad had told me and everything felt like it was coming together.

When I pulled in at the end of that first session, Dad was quite excited and started firing questions at me about the bike, but I was much more interested in his opinion of my performance. 'How do you think I did?' I kept pestering him.

He was his normal self and said, 'Don't worry about that, just tell me what the bike's doing. Is it OK on the brakes? Where can we make some improvements?' He changed the suspension a little bit to give me a slightly better feel for the damp conditions and we altered the gearing slightly as well. Then I went out for the second session and, with those changes to the bike, I was even faster.

One goal I had set myself was to get my knee down, which I hadn't been able to do at Donington because the bikes were so big and the footpegs so low. It's something you never do in motocross, which needs a completely different riding style, and it was why this experience was so alien to me. I'd seen heroes like Kevin Schwantz do it on TV so often and I knew it's a way riders gauge how far over the bike is leaning in a corner. It's a subconscious thing now, but I remember it being so important then, a little indication I could be a short-circuit racer.

It was probably like watching an elephant riding a bicycle, me at 70kg and 1.72m trying to find my way around a 125. But I got my knee down, scraping my virgin sliders as proof, and I loved it! It was satisfying to hit that little target, but it also told me how hard I was pushing and how close I was getting to the probable limits of grip.

I was beginning to think I had a real chance of making the cut and being one of the final five who the Red Bull Rookies team would take to Spain for a test.

Then I crashed.

Maybe I was getting a little too confident, but racing is all about finding the edge of performance and sometimes you have to go beyond the limit to find where the limit is. I was putting more and more lean angle into corners, but as I accelerated out of one left-hander, still banked over quite far, I went through a big damp patch. I'd seen it on previous laps but, as you carry more corner speed you run wider on corner exits and this time I couldn't avoid it. As my front tyre touched the edge of the damp patch it lost traction, the handlebars folded to the left and I fell off the inside of the bike. It was my first tarmac crash and I remember it lasted such a long time. When you crash a motocross bike, you just stop because you're on mud or sand and a part of your body or a part of the bike just digs in and the crash is over, often quite painfully. In this crash at Rockingham I wasn't hurt, but I just remember sliding. And sliding. And sliding.

I'd been a bit worried about crashing on tarmac, but I hadn't fallen very far off the bike and my dad's old leathers had done their job. When I eventually stopped I thought, 'Ah, that wasn't so bad!' But when I went to pick up the bike, I realised that the left handlebar and footpeg were broken.

First, I felt guilty about damaging Alan's bike, then I just felt stupid for crashing it in the first place. I managed to bump start the bike and ride it back to the pits, but it wasn't in any state for me to continue.

I was just devastated. I'd completely blown this one opportunity I had to continue racing. My heart sank at the thought of being remembered by that selection committee as the raw motocross kid who crashed in the third session of a selection day. So we sadly packed everything back into the van, saying nothing apart from our thanks and goodbyes and we set off with a shattered dream for the long drive north to catch the ferry from Cairnryan.

I felt I'd been quite fast for someone who had only ever ridden one day on a road bike. My only consolation was I still had this vague offer from Joe Millar back home in Ireland, and me and my dad started to talk about calling him as soon as we were back.

As we drove along the A75 towards Stranraer, my phone rang. I saw a number I didn't recognise. This voice said, 'Is that Jonathan?'

I should have recognised the team boss, Robin Appleyard, by the Yorkshire accent, but I wasn't thinking straight. I replied, 'Yes, who's this?'

He told me who he was and said, 'I just wondered what you thought of today's test at Rockingham.' I figured he was just after a bit of feedback on the day, so I said, 'Yeah, I thought it was well organised and I really enjoyed it until I crashed.' Then I thanked him for the opportunity and thought that would be it.

He said crashing was all part of the learning process. 'But I'm really pleased you enjoyed the day, Jonathan,' he said. 'Do you have a passport?' I hesitated and said, 'Er … yeah, I've got one at home.' He said, 'Well, that's good because you're going to need it in a couple of months. You're in our final five and you're coming to Spain for the final test.'

I just went through a complete 180-degree flip – from being devastated that the dream had been shattered to being absolutely elated that I was still in the game. Viva España – the little motocross kid from Northern Ireland, who'd never ridden a road bike, was in the Grand Final!

Before the test, scheduled for March, my dad and Alan Patterson agreed it would be a good idea to go to Cartagena, where the test was to be, to learn the track and spend a bit more time on that 125cc racing machine. So in February we set off for three days at the annual winter test for a lot of UK-based teams, organised by Barry Symmons, who had previously been Honda UK's racing manager. It turned out to be a complete eye-opener as to what happens on boys' trips away. Of course, as the saying has it, what goes on tour stays on tour, but there was a lot of stuff happening out there that you never see in Kilwaughter. I quickly learned that old Spanish hotels with flashing lights outside are not necessarily a disco or nightclub.

I felt I'd joined this exclusive club because all I'd known was schoolboy motocross. Now I was away in Spain, staying in a hotel, eating out, not having to power-wash bikes every day – and I was loving it!

I also got going really fast on the bike and was comparing well with a few guys there who had ridden at British championship level. Alan was great for me with all his two-stroke experience and taught me about setting up a gearbox and getting the carburation right on the bike. Instead of one day on a 500cc four stroke that I'd had before the Rockingham test, I had three and a half more days' experience and felt a lot more comfortable on the bike.

I didn't feel quite as good a month later, however, when I was on my own and away to the final Red Bull Rookies selection day, aged 16, without my parents or anyone familiar. Former GP rider Jeremy McWilliams, who was involved in the selection, had told Dad, 'You just need to let him go and don't be the schoolboy dad.'

I knew of the other four finalists – Ashley Beech, Daniel Cooper, Michael Robertson and Barry Burrell – who were all established riders, and of course there were team managers and mechanics who I was introduced to.

The bike I rode at the test was incredible. Not that Alan's 125 hadn't been good, but it was a bike he'd made for a customer. The Red Bull Hondas that Robin Appleyard had prepared were proper new high-end bikes. From what Alan had taught me, I was able to give some feedback on the first day and I was faster than all my rivals, as well as both Midge Smart and Guy Farbrother, the two existing riders in the team. In fact, they started coming to me to talk about set-up, asking me things like, 'Do you think second gear needs to be a bit shorter for that corner?'

I was surprised that I felt pretty comfortable without Dad there. I'd spent a lot of my childhood around adults in racing paddocks so I got on very well with all the mechanics at the test. I was just being myself and I felt so at home in this new environment – tarmac instead of dirt or sand, garages instead of awnings and a crew of professional technicians instead of enthusiastic and supportive relatives and friends. But I still heard my parents' voices in my head, telling me to be polite and respectful, so I made sure I thanked everyone for the opportunity. It felt like a big deal too; a TV crew was hovering around the track making a documentary. The whole test went incredibly well and I was thinking there was no way they couldn't pick me, because my lap times were so much faster than the others. And that's how it turned out – I remember phoning home and telling my dad, feeling so super-happy I could have cried. I was going to ride for the Red Bull Rookies Honda team in the British 125cc Championship.

It was a big thing. The championship provided support races for the British Superbike series, and the Red Bull Rookies Honda team was the one in the 125cc class that everyone wanted to ride for. The top Superbike riders like John Reynolds and Michael Rutter were household names. And there was me, getting ready to be a part of that giant circus.

In the first round, my first ever race on tarmac at Silverstone, I out-qualified both Midge and Guy in 12th and finished the race in the top 10.

If I ever thought Desertmartin was an impressive paddock, the number of motorhomes, 40ft trucks and hospitality units in the British Superbike paddock was incredible. I felt under a little bit of pressure, but there were never any expectations put on me by the team.

I was always going to be physically challenged on a 125. It wasn't just my height, it was the fact that I was built like a motocrosser – quite tall, muscular and broad in the upper body – which you could say is not ideal for a tiny little race bike. In fact, I'm the same weight today as I was in that first Red Bull season, and the bike I ride now is just a tad more powerful.

After that first race my results were a bit more sporadic but, at the penultimate round in September at Brands Hatch, I woke up to a dry, sunny race day. I had only qualified 12th on the grid – the wrong end of the third row – but I was feeling confident and there was always a good crowd at Brands, which fired me up to battle through the field. It's a really short lap on the Brands Indy circuit, around 50 seconds, but there were 24 laps and I managed to finish third, a couple of seconds down on Steven Neate and my team-mate Midge Smart, who won the race. Crossing the line for my first podium was the most amazing feeling, and I remember screaming into my helmet at the thought of spraying champagne in front of the Brands Hatch crowd, even though technically I was still too young to drink it.

I was still in my final year at Larne Grammar and had to find time for my GCSEs. When we were able, we travelled as a family and often used to get the Fleetwood-to-Larne boat back from a British championship round on a Sunday night; I remember one time early in the season my mum sitting me down in the boat cabin to get my coursework done before I went back to school the following morning.

Sometimes to save money on flights I stayed at Midge's house in Peterborough between races. He turned out to be extremely helpful during that season. He was from New Zealand, only a year older, but seemed a bit more worldly-wise. I was a raw 16-year-old kid, staying away from home on my own for the first time, so everything felt new and fresh and exciting. We'd stay up late talking about bikes and girls and he became a good friend.

I got a great schooling in racing that year – the technical features of a racing motorcycle and the more subtle aspects of racecraft – learning things that have stood me in good stead throughout my career. Robin Appleyard taught me more in that one year of 125 GP British Championship racing than I'd have learned in five doing it on my own. Things like setting up gearboxes and changing gear ratios for different corners on a track. Because I was a bigger rider he taught me ways to improve my corner exits – the positioning of the bike on the track and the positioning of my body on the bike – to carry more speed on to the next straight. I also learned that the British championship paddock took racing very seriously, I guess because everything cost more and there was basically more money at stake.

Robin was super-good but I realised, because of my size, I didn't have a realistic future in his team. I was desperate to carry on road racing, but some of the guys I was racing against were tiny – guys like Tommy Bridewell, who was so small he was like a baby. He certainly wasn't the fastest round corners, but he would drill us on straights and put 20m on me because of his weight. So on a 125, I was pissing upstream a lot of the time.

Towards the end of that season I started speaking with Linda Pelham, the marketing manager of Red Bull who was running the Rookies programmes, about what options I had. She said, 'Listen, don't worry. I'm trying to work on something,' but I had no idea what she had in mind. I started thinking about going back to motocross because, although I'd had a few decent results on the 125, they hadn't been enough for any other team to offer me a ride. We couldn't afford to buy a ride either, an option that had started to creep in at the time and which has become a reality of present-day opportunities. My dad had been right on his financial limit to do motocross, so that was going to be way out of reach. Tyres alone were so expensive.

The ideal next step was a ride in the Supersport class, which featured much bigger and more powerful 600cc four-stroke bikes. These were slightly tuned versions of models you could ride on the road, and formed a very important sales category for all the Japanese manufacturers. But I had absolutely no idea how I was going to convince any team to take on a motocross kid who had done a less-than-spectacular year on 125s.

CHAPTER 5

THE BIG BREAK

I REALLY WANTED to make the move up to Supersport, but it wasn't going to be easy. I'd made good friends in my first year in the British championship paddock, among them Superstock rider Stephen Thompson and his partner Charlotte Pullen, who often took me to the races in their truck. They knew I wanted to make the move up and they put us in touch with a guy called Nick Morgan at MSS Kawasaki. But there was a problem: he wanted £35,000 for the season. Back then we couldn't even think about coming up with that kind of money without help.

Talking things over with Red Bull's Linda Pelham, I stressed that even though I was only 16, I needed to make the move to a 600cc bike because of my size.

'I'm still working on some plans,' she told me. 'Don't commit to anything without speaking to me first.'

Another avenue we explored was with the Northern Ireland-based TAS Suzuki squad, run by Hector Neill and his son, Philip, who I knew a little from motocross. But they weren't remotely interested in me for the 2004 season; they were planning to hire Tom Sykes and Adrian Coates.

Then Linda came back to me. 'Look,' she said, 'I can't promise anything, but I really want to take this Red Bull Rookie thing to the next level and I've had a good meeting with Honda Racing.'

Linda had convinced Neil Tuxworth, the Honda Racing manager, to give me a try-out for a potential new junior team to be run out of Honda's HQ in Louth, Lincolnshire. It was to be a stepping stone from 125 racing to the Supersport class, with Honda providing the bikes, the team and the whole infrastructure. It was exactly what I needed.

Linda is tall and imposing and she probably intimidated Neil a bit – he was old-fashioned and not accustomed to women in the workplace. She has a light grasp of technical matters but knows what she wants, can be direct in conversations and she doesn't suffer fools.

She had pleaded with him to at least give me a go, telling him he had nothing to lose. It was going to be another selection day and I was going to have to learn to ride another new bike and prove myself all over again. Only later did I find out Neil had virtually ruled me out before I even got there. He thought I wasn't going to be fast enough, because I didn't have enough experience after just a single season racing 125s.

The try-out was at Cadwell Park, five miles south of Louth, on another cold and damp end-of-season November day, just like the Red Bull selection the year before.

There were four of us competing for a Supersport ride on the expanded Red Bull Rookies Honda team: me, Kieran Clarke, Daniel Coutts and Cal Crutchlow. These guys had all been short-circuit racing for years. I had raced against Daniel before, as he'd been a regular podium finisher with the Padgetts team in the British 125 series. Kieran and Cal were a bit older and had both won 600cc races in the Yamaha R6 Cup, a one-make British Supersport feeder series.

At the track, Linda and her Red Bull colleague Ariane Frank may have been rooting for me to win the spot, but they were having to be very discreet about it. Although Red Bull were joining forces with Honda, the whole set-up was very much on Honda's terms. And what a set-up it was. I'd thought our Red Bull Rookies' 17-ton truck had been impressive, but this was another level. The amazing Honda Racing truck was crawling with technicians, and media interest in the day was being managed by a slick PR firm. There were interviews to see how marketable you were, which I think I handled pretty well. Those make-believe post-race interviews were starting to pay off.

We also met the crew. One bike was looked after by Chris Pike, the project's manager and my future crew chief, while an Aussie technician called Tommy Larson was in charge of the other. I spent a long time with Tommy and we really hit it off.

I was starting to find out about the next level and of how much input a rider could and should have on what gets done to a bike. One of the most important things we discuss is getting the balance of the bike, or the weight distribution, right. It can be affected by ride height, which, put simply, raises or lowers the bike in relation to the track surface. If you raise the rear, you put more weight on the front of the bike, which makes it turn better, but you sacrifice a bit of stability. It's always a compromise between stability and agility. After that we might talk about adjusting the weight of the springs in the front forks or the rear shock, and then fine-tune the suspension with preload or compression and rebound damping. When we've found a compromise on the chassis, then we'll look at electronics, and how much engine braking or traction control we want, for example. From the 125 that season, I was familiar with working on the balance of the bike or getting the correct gear ratios for the best combination of acceleration out of corners and top speed on the straights, but electronics was all new to me.

I hit it off with the CBR600RR immediately. It felt fast straight away, and if Robin Appleyard's 125s were great little race bikes, these things were works of art. It suited my physique so much better and everything was brand new, bits of carbon fibre everywhere, and a real trick bike that Supersport legend Karl Harris had ridden to the British championship title that season.

During the sessions, I tried to use a bit of common sense and build up my pace steadily, learning the bike and trying not to crash. After each run, I asked Tommy for a few positive technical changes, and that meant step-by-step I went faster by being able to open the throttle earlier out of corners, gaining more stability under braking or finding the bike easier to turn in, to nail an apex. Each session, I was able to ride a bit more aggressively and use that extra power I could feel being unleashed by my right hand.

By the end of the day, I was the quickest of the four riders and Neil Tuxworth had to sit up and take notice. As I left Cadwell that evening, I knew I'd got the gig: selected to ride in the 2004 British Supersport Championship.

Before I really understood what was happening, I had to fly to Italy to get measured up for new leathers and boots at some Italian manufacturers the team had a sponsorship deal with. I hadn't been abroad since the Red Bull Rookies 125 test, back when I was still wearing Dad's leathers. And here I was, being given a full guided tour of the factory, watching the guys cutting and sewing jackets and racing suits. I thought, 'Bloody hell, I've arrived. I'm a factory rider.'

Back in the UK, right next door to my Red Bull team workshop in Louth was the official Honda Racing BSB squad with Michael Rutter and Ryuichi Kiyonari, plus the reigning British Supersport champion Karl Harris. This was another level again. Luckily, at the same time Honda took over my old Red Bull Rookies 125 team with my friends Eugene Laverty and Steven Neate now riding with them. Having Eugene in the amalgamated Honda team was a huge help: I was still only 17 and it was great to see a familiar face from back home.

Winter testing in Spain gave me another opportunity to ride the CBR600RR and learn how the bigger heavier bike needed to be ridden. Those familiar British circuits would feel very different on a bike producing 140bhp instead of 40bhp. The step up to a Supersport machine was even bigger than the move from motocross to 125. Suddenly these bikes were animals that could bite you. When you're travelling at 170mph, the smallest touch on the handlebars can have a dramatic effect. Your braking has to be so precise, and you have to learn exactly how quickly you can get on the gas out of a corner or how to set up the front of the bike to get more stability under braking.

On a 125, it was so important to maintain corner speed because of the slower acceleration. The Supersport bike was much more powerful, so I needed to be a little more careful: if I opened the throttle too soon the rear tyre would lose grip and spin. That meant either no forward progress or, in the worst case, a crash. All this while racing in close proximity to other bikes whose riders are fighting for exactly the same piece of tarmac and trying to control their own machines in the same way. Racing is not meant to be a contact sport, but that doesn't stop riders banging knees and elbows or swapping paint, and many's the time I've come in after a race with someone else's tyre marks on my leathers.

I was getting ready to battle against a lot of top-level stars. Former world championship riders Jay Vincent, Adrian Coates and Pere Riba; the other young guns like Tom Sykes, Leon Camier and Cal Crutchlow; and then there was Karl Harris, one of the most naturally gifted riders I ever saw.

Karl was built like a middleweight boxer so had a natural physique for a middleweight bike like a 600cc Supersport machine. He seemed like he could roll out of bed into his leathers and still outperform a rider on equal machinery who spent his entire life in the gym trying to get stronger or improve his riding technique. His natural skill set allowed him to get the most out of life away from the track, too – he certainly liked to party.

For the first round at Silverstone, I qualified 10th and finished 12th in the race. In the second round at Brands Hatch, I was running in the top six near the end of the race but crashed out, and then crashed again in the next race at Snetterton when I fell on oil left by another bike on the track. Then I had a brake failure in practice at Oulton Park, caused by a mechanical oversight, which led to me being knocked out in the crash and missing the race.

The early races of that season were another big learning curve, I enjoyed some good battles and was confident enough of being able to hold my own. But overall, I hadn't had the greatest start to my first season in this ultra-competitive class, with no points in three of the first four races.

The next three rounds were better, though, and by mid-season I had started to find my feet. My best result was in early June at Thruxton, in Hampshire, where I got involved in a great scrap with the third group in the race. It was my first visit to this old airfield circuit on the 600, which had about 100bhp more than the 125 I rode the previous season. It's one of the fastest circuits on the BSB calendar and after the 125, the Supersport bike felt like switching to warp speed. The right-hander Church Corner is fourth gear, flat-out and leads on to a long straight where slip-streaming becomes really important for the final part of the lap. Pere Riba, who is now my crew chief in World Superbikes, was about five seconds up the road in fifth while I got into a great scrap with ex-250 GP rider Jay

Vincent, along with Paul Young, Shane Norval and Tom Sykes on the TAS Suzuki. I was able to use my slip-streaming experience from 125s to get to the front of the group and I was very satisfied to win that particular little battle. I think the four of us were covered by about 1.5s at the line, with me in sixth and Tom finishing tenth.

My confidence was improving with every race as I learned more about the bike. I was continuing to adapt my riding style and I started to get the measure of my competitors. I was feeling very positive for the second half of the season.

Then we went to Knockhill in Scotland for the eighth round, and everything changed.

It was 4 July, race day. I'd qualified 10th the day before and was riding confidently on my out-lap for morning warm-up to confirm our settings for the afternoon's race. Knockhill is a very short circuit – about 1.3 miles – but you can build up speed to about 160mph climbing the start-finish straight. As I completed my out-lap and started my first flying lap, I was coming towards the downhill right-hander at the end of the straight, popping up from under the screen and getting ready to change down four gears into second.

We use braking points on track – the latest possible point at which you feel comfortable braking and stopping effectively enough to tip into the apex of a corner. The bite of the front brake is always instant, so as soon as you touch the lever you feel the pressure and get an idea of how you're going to manage the braking – a little more if you're entering the corner faster, for example, or releasing it earlier if you're carrying a little less speed.

I touched the brake. There was nothing. No pressure at all. The lever came all the way back to my handlebar.

By then I was already past the braking point to make the corner.

I was genuinely frightened for my life, because there's very little run-off in turn one at Knockhill and I knew how close the tyre wall and barrier were to the track. I had so little time to think and, with hindsight, the better strategy might have been to jump off the bike immediately and use my leathers on the tarmac and then in the gravel to slow me down. In my panic though, the instinct was to cover the rear brake a little and back-shift an extra gear to take some speed off.

These thoughts were going through my head over the space of about 25 metres at around 150mph, by which time I was at the gravel trap.

I was entering the gravel at full lean angle and it was way too late to jump off. I thought that if I could go into the gravel with the bike on its side, maybe I could avoid the tyre wall. I closed my eyes but before I had time for another thought I had hit the tyre wall.

Everything went quiet and I couldn't properly see straight. My body went completely numb but very warm at the same time. I knew something bad had happened, but I wasn't sure what.

Unfortunately, I wasn't knocked out. I was pretty aware of the pain and of everything that was going on around me. I heard the paramedic say, 'He's broken his femur.' The femur is the biggest and toughest bone in the body, stronger, they say, than concrete. I asked the paramedic later how he knew and he told me it was because my leg was bent side-ways, about halfway down my femur, and pointing in completely the wrong direction. That'd do it.

I can't remember too much more apart from people bend-ing over me and someone injecting me with something in my arm as they were explaining what was going to happen next. Whatever they put in me made me feel even warmer, particu-larly my leg, which had a lot of pain, but that started to go away. It came back when there was a bit of a kerfuffle getting me onto a spinal board and then a stretcher. I could feel the top of my leg moving, but I couldn't feel the bottom at all. It felt like someone had inflated my leg to about 1,000psi of pressure while the rest of my body was shutting down, almost deflating.

I felt somehow detached from what was going on – like I was in some kind of trance – and I don't remember speaking at all, I just let everything happen to me and was happy to let these people take control. Because it was faster than using the access roads, we went the wrong way back up the track in the ambulance to the medical centre where I was stabi-lised a little more.

My parents were there first, then the team manager Havier Beltran arrived. 'Those fucking brakes failed again!' I yelled at Harv. All I could think was that the brake failure had been caused by another mechanical oversight, like a nut that hadn't been tightened correctly. It was the exact same thing that had happened at Oulton Park four races before.

I think that was the first time my parents ever heard me swear.

Left: Hanging out on the Isle of Man TT Grandstand, watching Dad do his thing.

Right: My first race didn't last long. The little PW got water in the electrics and stopped.

Left: Three generations of the Rea family (plus Joe Millar) – my Granda John on the left, my dad Johnny in the middle and me as a baby on his bike.

Focused on winning the three-legged race, at Ballynure Primary School sports day, with Philip.

I loved this little KX60 so much, and it kick-started my obsession with winning.

Receiving my award for winning the 60cc British Motocross Championship aged 10.

Trying to get a 70kg, 5ft 7in frame tucked up on that 125cc bike wasn't easy.

Trying not to look like a motocross rider on my first road race experience at the Ron Haslam Race School.

Jeremy McWilliams has always been a good sounding board. This was at the Red Bull Selection event in Cartagena, 2003.

My 2004 Supersport season didn't last long but I had some great battles. Here with Michael Laverty, Pere Riba and Tom Sykes.

Right: Getting another ticking off from Havier Beltran. I'd a lot to learn, I suppose.

Right: Having fun over the famous Cadwell Park Mountain.

Left: Mondello Park, 2005 – I became the youngest ever rider to secure a BSB pole position at the age of 18.

Left: I learned a lot from Neil Tuxworth – especially the importance of being on time.

Right: Out of the shadows and into the light, 2007 was a breakthrough year where I challenged for the British Superbike title right to the last round with Ryuichi Kiyonari.

Left: My first BSB win meant so much, particularly as it came at my home round of Mondello Park.

Left: Battling with Andrew Pitt and travelling the world at the age of 21 in the World Supersport Championship was pretty epic.

Right: My rookie Superbike season didn't get off to the best start I threw a few toys out of the pram after this race in Valencia.

Left: I didn't have to wait long for my first SBK win. Here with Ronald ten Kate after winning at Misano, 2009.

Getting the call-up to replace Casey Stoner for a few races in MotoGP. I went 8–7 after juggling GP and SBK back-to-back for five weeks.

Two days after breaking my femur, the doctor had me out of bed and walking.

Marrying my best friend, in the Lake District, July 2012.

Right: Spending a summer in Australia with Andrew Pitt and his family, with plenty of good times!

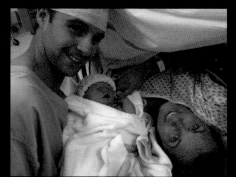

Left: Welcome to the world, Jake Elijah Rea. This pic went viral as E! News had mistaken Tatia for some celebrity.

My leg was a real mess. I had multiple fractures high up the bone near my hip. I was in bits emotionally too. I was transferred to Dunfermline's Queen Margaret Hospital. X-rays showed I'd also broken my ankle and I went straight into the operating theatre that night. Over seven hours they separated the broken femur from my knee and drilled through the bone to thread a long pin up the middle, which was then fixed in place by three screws, two in the knee and one in the hip. I'd lost so much blood that I needed three transfusions.

I spent three weeks in Dunfermline, made a little easier by Darren Wilson, an old motocross friend, who gave my mum somewhere to stay and lent her a car so she could visit every day. I was a 17-year-old kid, fresh out of school.

When I finally got back home, I started the long road of rehab. I spent a lot of lonely days in a hyperbaric chamber in Larne which was normally used for divers suffering from 'the bends'. Mum or Dad used to take me up there every day for two-hour sessions in this pressurised tank where I breathed 100% oxygen to get oxygenated blood to the site of the injury and speed up the healing process. It was a five-seater tank that looked a bit like a mini-submarine, with a TV screen on the outside showing crappy daytime TV like *The Jeremy Kyle Show*.

This was in the days before the iPhone had been invented, kids. I spent every single day of my life in this metal box, trying to treat it like a job, but it started to get to me. After a while, I couldn't help dwelling on what was happening to my life, asking myself what the hell I was doing there and wondering whether my career was over before it had even begun. I was sitting there because of someone else's mistake, not because of anything I'd done, and all kinds of thoughts went through my head – anger, bitterness, self-pity.

I had no money and the little the insurance policy had paid out – maybe £1,000 – was going on physiotherapy. I just felt useless. Spending two hours every day of the week in that fucking tube, watching Jeremy Kyle, was enough to drive anyone mental. I hadn't done enough or got good enough results to prove myself on the bike. I'd just left school having only ever considered one career option and that dream was over. I had to try and fight these thoughts, to be as positive as I could, and to think that my leg was going to get better and stronger again, that I would get back on track and battle my British Supersport rivals again. But it was often difficult to focus on that, and the temptation to go back to the negative thoughts was never far away.

All the meetings I had every few weeks with specialists and consultants told me that there was no evidence of bone growth and that I'd maybe need another operation. It felt like there was nothing positive ever happening. And being away from the track was difficult, too, knowing how quickly you're forgotten when you're not there. When you're doing well, you get back to your motorhome after a race to find 50 messages from friends and family trying to get through on your phone; but back then there was just radio silence and it seemed like no-one was interested in how I was doing or wanting to take me out for a beer. I felt damaged mentally as well as physically, and the feelings of loneliness and help-lessness were overpowering sometimes.

For a while, I wasn't interested in getting up in the morning, it was a real chore to try to get fit again. That light at the end of the tunnel flickered for a while then it just stopped being there when I woke up. I had some pretty black days.

Eventually, they decided I did need that second operation, almost three months after the first. So, at the end of September, they re-drilled through the bone and inserted a new pin to try to wake up the cells around the injury site and stimulate the bone growth.

I was in hospital recovering from that operation when Neil Tuxworth and Linda Pelham came to see me. I was still feeling pretty sorry for myself and I was not the best company. I'd been following all the race results, seeing what I was missing out on, and I was in regular contact with a few guys in the paddock. But Neil wasn't top of the list of people I wanted to visit me: he was the representative of the fledg-ling racing career I feared I had lost.

I sat up in bed and asked politely how the guys in the team were doing and we made a bit of small talk, which I'm never very good at.

Then Neil said, 'Linda and I are keen to see how you are recovering because, if everything goes OK and your rehab goes well, we were planning to put you up to the British Superbike championship junior team next year.'

I stared at each of them in turn, looking for some sign that they were joking, or that I was dreaming. But I could see they meant it. They wanted me riding a Honda Fireblade in British Superbikes.

I didn't know what to say. I blubbered, 'Thank you.'

Suddenly, that light at the end of the tunnel began to more than flicker. To go from feeling so completely down and out to having this incredible carrot dangled in front of me was something I couldn't quite get my head around. Now I had every reason to get up in the morning and go to work on my strength and fitness.

I knew that as soon as I got the green light after the second operation I'd be working flat out on a conditioning and physio programme. I couldn't wait, and the confidence that Neil and Linda had shown gave me an incredible amount of hope. Of course, first I had to check my femur was growing back properly. So, a few weeks later on a bright and breezy Belfast day in November, I was sitting in a waiting room at the Royal Victoria Hospital with my good friend and Red Bull's athlete performance manager Darren Roberts. I was still buzzing from Neil and Linda's visit, and since then Darren and I had been working on every area of my fitness apart from my leg.

The orthopaedic surgeon called me in. I'll never forget the look on his face: cold and hard. Expressionless.

I chirped in: 'So, when do you think I can be ready for winter testing?'

He asked me to sit down, went through some pleasantries, and then he read his notes and studied an X-ray for a while without saying anything.

He looked across at me over the top of his glasses and said, 'I'm afraid there won't be any winter testing. In fact, there can't be any more racing or riding bikes at all. I'm sorry Jonathan, but my professional opinion is that your leg will never be strong enough to survive another crash. You can't ride again.'

The second operation hadn't worked. The bone cells hadn't woken up sufficiently and there had been no significant growth in the gap that remained in the bone. If he had said all that before Linda and Neil's visit, who knows what effect that would have had on me. But now, instead of crashing back down to reality, I almost didn't hear what he was saying. It was just a kind of noise, an interference.

It certainly wasn't going to shake me from my belief that I would be on the grid for the start of the 2005 British Superbike championship. Nothing – not even an orthopaedic surgeon giving me news like that – was going to stop me.

Of course, we still had to do what we could to get the bone growing again. At the beginning of December, I went into surgery for a third time, to have a piece of bone from my hip grafted onto the huge gap in my femur. This time it worked.

As weird as it sounds, being told by the consultant that I wouldn't ride again had fired me up more than anything. That promise from Red Bull Honda gave me the belief; it was the only incentive I needed to get fit again. Not only was that third operation successful, the motivation to get back to full fitness was still there and stronger than ever.

Because of Linda and Red Bull, I had Darren pretty much at my disposal during that whole period. He visited me in Ballyboley where we spent countless hours working on my strength and the range of motion in my knee. Project Rebuild was unbelievably tough and I had to push myself to the limits of my strength, endurance and pain threshold.

I spent time with Darren in Manchester and he'd come and stay with me and we'd do a lot of seated boxing to keep my core strength as high as possible. But what we worked on the most was improving the range of movement in my knee, because every time they'd gone into my femur during an operation it would sustain even more damage, on top of an old motocross injury. There was always a lot of fluid in there from the trauma caused by the screws holding the pin in place, and even though I was encouraged to walk and put pressure through the metalwork in my femur, it was agony to bend my knee and any walking I did just inflamed it all again.

It was a constant circle of physio, exercise and icing and we got through a load of training, but there was only so much fitness work I could do without using my legs. Darren had done a lot of rehabilitation with other athletes and while I was staying with him I worked with some of the Salford rugby league guys as they were coming back from injury.

Darren also helped me out with all his experience of the emotional side of rehabilitation, the periods of doubt that any sportsperson goes through during the comeback process, wondering whether they'll ever perform at the same level again. But he wasn't a shoulder to cry on; he was always very matter of fact and practical about it, which worked well with me. I started to feel like less of a victim and more like a professional sportsperson going through something that is just part of the job. That period changed my whole attitude to injury recovery and served me well in the years to come. I felt like I was genuinely preparing myself physically and mentally to become a Superbike rider.

CHAPTER 6

SECOND CHANCE

WE BEGAN WINTER testing in Spain just four months after being told I would never race again, and three months after that third operation.

Even leaving aside the fact I hadn't ridden for eight months, adjusting to the technical side of Superbike racing was another massive leap to make. It called for a radical change in the way I thought about the set-up of the bike, electronics, geometry, suspension and tyres.

The British Superbike Championship is 13 rounds with two races at each, so 26 races during the season at circuits all over the UK and Ireland, from Knockhill in Scotland to Thruxton in Hampshire and from Snetterton in the east to Dublin's Mondello Park in the west. It starts in April, which can be freezing and wet in the UK, and ends in October, which can also be freezing and wet. But we got some decent weather as well, occasionally.

As the team had a sponsorship deal with manufacturers, I got free leathers and boots, but I wasn't earning any salary nor was I on any kind of win or podium bonus, and the BSB Championship didn't pay out anything in prize money. So, although the Superbike ride was free, I had to cover my travelling expenses, which racked up a bit since all rounds except Mondello were over the water for me.

Back home by now, I was working at a very modest £3.20 an hour for an uncle of mine, my mum's brother-in-law Cecil, who ran a steel erecting business called Warwick Engineering. I was also doing a course in manufacturing engineering at Ballymena Technical College.

I used to ride to Warwick Engineering on a 50cc scooter and I remember getting a hairline fracture in my ankle after crashing in a Supercross race one winter and having to wear an airboot. It was snowing and freezing cold, but Mum made me ride to work. It was that slippery, I kept both feet down pretty much the whole way to work, but I still crashed about three times. In fair weather, though, getting to work was always a race, firstly because I never got out of bed until the last possible moment, and secondly because I enjoyed racing the clock on the way in. So it was the backroads of Ballyboley that taught me the art of aerodynamics.

My Uncle Cecil was a legend and I was really grateful for the job and the flexibility he gave me to go racing, but it was hilarious hearing how the workers would talk about him and hang shit on him all the time, the way people everywhere do about their bosses. I was treated the same as everyone else and the best days were when we were called out on site to erect the steelwork, like installing metal handrails or bannisters in a house. We'd always stop on the way to pick up breakfast, which was usually soda bread filled with egg, sausage, bacon and onions.

From the ages of 16 to about 18, going to work every day turned into another great adventure, and I was working with guys who were a lot older than me which taught me some colourful language and a few other things besides.

Meanwhile, my ride with Red Bull Honda was an opportunity to put myself in the shop window and show what I was capable of. These days, it's much more common for young riders or their parents to pay for a ride and, theoretically, the more you pay the better package you'll get. Those kinds of deals were just starting to come in back then, so I felt incredibly lucky to be being given this chance.

My Honda CBR1000RR Fireblade was anything but 'factory'. It was a project bike with a powerful engine and electronics that made the power delivery a bit like a light switch – either on or off. Not ideal for the narrow circuits of the British Superbike championship.

After three successive seasons of promotion, I was now lining up in the premiership of British bike racing, against some of the biggest names: Ryuichi Kiyonari, Jeremy McWilliams, Leon Haslam, Sean Emmett, Gregorio Lavilla, Michael Rutter, Karl Harris and others. These were guys who I'd been watching for years, riders from Grand Prix and World Superbikes.

OK, I had strong self-belief, and I was sure I was there on merit, but this was daunting.

I was also struggling emotionally. I was getting over a bad leg break, was fresh out of school and had nobody embracing me. I know very well, even today, I need that from time to time. I was also still in this no-man's land, wondering whether I should be working for a living to fund my dream or become a full-time professional motorcycle racer. I just ended up stuck in the middle of the two, commuting back and forth between races or sleeping on friends' couches. The dream of riding professionally was so close, and I was competing against guys who had been doing it for years. But I was a working man back home. While Uncle Cecil was incredibly flexible and generous to let me go racing, I needed to give the sport everything.

The early months of the season were incredibly tough as I struggled to understand the range of settings available on a Superbike and how the tyre went off during a 20- or 25-lap race. The leg didn't help. Muscling a 165kg Superbike around is demanding on the body, especially the arms and legs as you shift your balance from one side of the bike to the other. It's only on the straights, where you crouch down under the screen, that you get any respite.

In my first race of the season at Brands Hatch, I managed to score some points, and by round four I was starting to break into the top ten occasionally. I had some highlights, like qualifying on the front row at Croft, where I was a couple of tenths behind Michael Rutter on pole, and I was ahead of the other Honda riders, Ryuichi Kiyonari and Karl Harris, and beginning to feel like I was competitive with them, even though they were on better equipment.

All the same, good race results were hard to come by. I wanted to be at the sharp end, being really competitive, and I just wasn't.

I began to think that I'd maybe bitten off a bit more than I could chew. I'm sure it was tricky for the team's management to justify the results to their bosses, because although I definitely had potential, in reality I wasn't doing well enough. I was young and raw, maybe still slightly immature. But I think in the back of all our minds there was also this unspoken feeling that I'd nearly had my career ended prematurely by having my brakes fail twice due to human oversight. I guess I was feeling that the very least I deserved was a bit of patience.

By the time I got back to Knockhill I'd been through so many operations, so much rehab, so many extreme emotions that it didn't really matter where I'd broken my leg. I hadn't forgotten about it, but I'd parked the experience and the emotion that went with it, which allowed me to concentrate on what I was there to do.

Then, at my home round at Mondello Park, about 45km west of Dublin, I became the youngest ever rider to start a BSB race from pole position, which made me hugely proud in front of a lot of friends and family who had made the two-hour trip down from the north. It was a timely reminder to me that I was where I belonged.

By the end of 2005, I was starting to go OK on the bike and understanding it better, so I could put some good laps together. As well as that pole position, I'd had fastest laps during races and I went quick during testing.

But things still weren't quite right off the track.

The Honda Racing Corporation – or HRC – is a subsidiary of the Honda Motor business in Japan dedicated exclusively to racing. They had returned to the British Superbike Championship for the 2005 season to support Japanese hero Ryuichi Kiyonari.

At the same time, Red Bull was paying Honda heaps of money to run this junior programme, but nobody on the team seemed to give a shit about me personally or know how to look after the human side of things. They would happily discuss technical aspects of the bike or share a Sunday night beer with me, but when it came to trying to understand how I worked or how they might get the best out of me as a rider, there seemed to be this emotional detachment.

Little things that should have been easy suddenly became hard, like helping me get a Honda motocross bike, which I still enjoyed riding, plus maybe some parts or kit. Asking for any kind of a favour was discouraged. At the same time, I could see how well riders in other teams were being treated and how much they were valued.

I was butting heads with team manager Havier 'Harv' Beltran. We had conflicting opinions about the bike and I was quite critical about it at times. But Harv always treated me like a little kid; I knew nothing and should just listen to the more experienced voices. I felt I'd shown I was learning; my opinion should have had some value. I didn't need to be patronised, I needed support and encouragement.

Neil Tuxworth was no better in showing that I was valued. Neil is a born and bred Lincolnshire man, an accomplished ex-racer and very regimented running a race team and managing budgets. He's also a real technophobe, still using a Nokia 3210 when everyone else was on their third or fourth smartphone.

He was always the boss and never interested in socialising, whereas at least Harv wanted to take me out for a beer when we weren't racing. Neil oversaw everything in the team. He's a strange and complex man but a brilliant boss. Over the years, I've flat-out disagreed with what he's saying in meetings and at other times he's given me a real bollocking and pulled me up on mistakes, but I've respected him for having the balls to do that.

He is also a master manipulator, but I can't hold anything against him – he's got Honda's blood running through his veins. He did an incredible job for the company until he retired at the end of 2017 and I really liked him, even though his reputation for being super-tight was totally justified.

Once, as Eugene and I were checking in at the hotel reception for a test at Snetterton in Norfolk, we bumped into Harv and he said, 'Do you fancy joining us for dinner?' Our eyes lit up and we all nodded enthusiastically, so we all met later in the hotel restaurant. Eugene and I sat opposite each other at one end of the table and went through the menu, which was way above and beyond the budgets of a couple of teenagers from Northern Ireland. We just filled our boots with prawn cocktail starters, steak for a main course and then some massive banana split or something for dessert, plus a load of Coke and Sprite to wash the meal down. There was no messing about with tap water, this was the full works.

We were having a great time, talking about our motocross days and reflecting on how amazing it was to be with the official Honda team in BSB. At the end of the evening, the waiter set the bill down in front of Neil. Then a little while later, he brought another bill and set it down in front of us. Neil was expecting us to split the bill. It was about forty quid each. And there's us without a pot to piss in.

We stared at each other like a couple of slapped puppies as we passed the bill back and forth, whispering to each other, 'Ask him!' 'No, you ask him!'

Eventually, I plucked up the courage and said, 'Neil, do we have to pay for this ourselves?' He replied, laughing to the other guys in the team, 'Of course, Jonathan, there's no such thing as a free lunch! Honda's not made of money and racing's certainly not cheap.'

We managed to scrape enough together with our cash and a card.

I learned two lessons very quickly: if you're asked out to dinner, check who's paying. And, if you want something done, don't bother going through Neil or Harv.

Over the season, I was also beginning to enjoy the other benefits of the sport: beers after the race, nights out here and there, partying and hanging out with chicks. In this I didn't exactly have responsible role models. Karl Harris enjoyed a drink or two and loved partying. Michael Rutter didn't have quite the same level of natural riding ability as Karl, but he was certainly happy enough to join in the party games. It seemed like we couldn't do any kind of PR event without drinking the hotel bar dry. Then there was Kiyo, a Japanese rider away from home, a closet smoker who loved a whisky. When sober he was quiet and reserved and there was always a language barrier, but his English was better when he was drunk and he became the life and soul of the party. In the gym, he spent hours stretching but didn't do a lot of real training. He was also obsessively clean and slept all the time.

They were all just normal blokes who happened to be very good at racing motorbikes, but it's probably fair to say none of them would have been a candidate for a *Men's Fitness* cover shoot. While I was a little surprised by the off-track activities, it wasn't completely alien to me because my early years were spent with Dad in road racing paddocks with guys like Joey Dunlop, who liked a beer.

But the impression I was getting from BSB was that you could win on Sunday and get hammered until Monday. It seemed relatively easy to earn yourself a nice six-figure salary, get a lot of national media coverage and have a pretty comfortable life from year to year. Because of those comfort levels, you needed quite a lot of ambition to make the next step.

I was never interested in staying in BSB just to try to win the championship there. As far as I was concerned, it was a stepping stone, a classroom to learn as much as I could, as quickly as I could. From my earliest motocross days, I wanted to be a world champion like Granda said – and that ambition had now been transferred to road racing. And you can't become a world champion in a national championship.

When the World Superbike Championship came to Donington Park I thought it was time to talk to some of their team managers about opportunities in their paddock.

But they weren't really interested in the British championship or what I was doing there. The world would have to wait.

THINGS REALLY STARTED to turn around in the 2006 season. Linda Pelham told me her dream had been to turn a kid who'd never seriously ridden a bike into a champion. Perhaps sensing that my time was coming, the support from her and Red Bull increased massively.

I was still in the junior team, below Kiyonari and Harris in the official outfit, but I started to feel the effect of HRC's involvement because the CBR machine for that season was a completely different animal. I was on a kit version, with upgraded electronics and parts bought from Japan to replicate the official factory bikes. We had top-quality Showa suspension, better than the WP kit we used the year before. So, although I was racing in the same class, there was a huge step up in the bike's performance. It was much easier to ride, and the throttle connection and fuel mapping were so much more precise and accurate. Instead of feeling like the bike wanted to rip my arms out every time I opened the throttle, the 2006 version felt much more tame, which inspired a lot of confidence, and I felt able to ride in anger and boss the bike instead of being scared of it. It made the races much easier physically, and instead of dedicating a load of brain power to thinking about opening and closing the throttle with as much finesse as I could, worrying about how it would react, I found the new bike much more predictable and easy to manage. It allowed me to concentrate on the riding, which made the races much more fun and much less tiring.

I still wasn't being paid by Honda, but I was trying to be as professional as I could. I stopped working at Warwick Engineering so I could dedicate myself 100% to racing motorcycles, and I rented a house in Louth with the mechanics so I could build a stronger relationship with them. It was a typical lads' house, with piles of washing-up and dirty clothes lying around, but we had a lot of laughs together. The relationships did get closer, but I had to go home regularly with a pile of laundry for my mum.

Louth is a very strange little town in deepest Lincolnshire and I have no idea how Neil Tuxworth sold the idea to Honda that they should set up their race headquarters there. He thinks geographically it's the centre of the universe, but honestly it isn't the centre of anything. It's more like a three-day camel ride from anywhere and nothing civilised ever goes on anywhere near. But it was great for me to be there.

I was getting talked about as a good prospect by the media, especially back home in Northern Ireland where, until that point, Michael Laverty had been the main focus of attention for short-circuit racing in papers like the *Belfast Telegraph* and the glossy monthly magazine *Irish Racer*. That was run by Paul Lindsay, who did so much for Irish motor racing, not only with the magazine but by hosting an annual black-tie awards where I was lucky enough to pick up a few trophies. Jeremy McWilliams, also from Northern Ireland, had just retired from Grand Prix racing so, as my results began to improve in BSB, the spotlight started to fall on me a bit more. I was getting more interview requests from the paddock media like *MCN*, and Eurosport became more interested in my views and future plans too. I was the young up-and-coming Superbike rider with no real experience but who people were beginning to tip as a future champion, possibly as soon as the following year.

Partly because of all that, I was offered a small sponsorship retainer from Alpinestars and some cash from Arai helmets. It was nothing spectacular and it didn't give me an extravagant lifestyle. I was lucky enough that my dad was also able to pay me a small wage for helping out on deliveries between races, so I could pay my bills. He also gave me a fuel card which made things a lot easier with the big mileage between circuits.

The team started to take a bit more notice of my opinion about the bike and we began to pull some results in. I took pole at Knockhill and Croft, and converted those into podium finishes, before scoring another at Cadwell Park. Standing on the British Superbike podium was incredibly special. I was 19 and each time I got to spray champagne up there with guys I'd admired for so long, I got more motivated to keep improving. I was learning more with each race and the team was growing more confident in my ability and my feedback.

Working with Chris Pike and Javier Gonzales, my suspension technician, I was learning about different ways to ride the bike. They had worked with riders like Kiyonari and two-time World Superbike champion, Colin Edwards, so they gave me some insight into their throttle and braking techniques. I was able to take it in, compute it in my brain and then transfer that to my bike. Until then, I had hardly ever used the rear brake on corner entry, but they both sat me down at one test and went through the benefits of using it – the way it allows the bike to settle and stabilise before applying the massive power of the front brake. It didn't come naturally at first and, with my size 10 feet, it was difficult to be subtle about it, but I learned to be gentle with the lever and now it has become second nature.

I also learned to manage tyre conservation because, with more than 200bhp, the rear tyres lose grip levels towards the end of races to the extent that they start spinning when you apply the throttle. I learned how to steer the bike with the rear wheel without destroying the tyre.

My race management also improved as I learned when to push to the maximum to make a pass or, perhaps, to hold back for a few laps in order to decide where and when would be best to make a move. My decision-making got better and better with each race.

I was learning about consistency as well, becoming more precise and accurate in my riding and maintaining good pace throughout the race, not just in short bursts. I also set about studying our pace compared to our rivals and recognising a realistic result that we could expect to achieve – finishing races and taking the points that were on offer, rather than crashing in trying to go for something better. As the season progressed, I became a regular finisher in the top five. Another podium at Brands Hatch in the final race resulted in me finishing fourth overall in the championship – the direct benefit of that consistency. I beat Karl and also Shane 'Shakey' Byrne, who had just returned from MotoGP, as well as a few other big names.

By the end of that season, I had become hot property and I was getting calls from Paul Denning at Crescent Suzuki, Colin Wright at GSE Ducati and Paul 'Birdy' Bird from Stobart Honda, who all wanted to talk about me riding their bikes the following year. At the same time, Neil Tuxworth was using his legendary manipulating and negotiating skills to try to convince me that signing a deal to move up to the official Honda team in 2007 was the best thing for my life and career.

Linda announced the Red Bull programme was going to close because, as she said, 'Our work here is done.' Although I still hadn't won a Superbike race, in the space of four years she had fulfilled her objective of taking a complete rookie kid all the way. Eugene was going to 250cc GPs and it looked like I was moving up to a professional BSB team.

As if to confirm my new status, Honda invited me to ride at the traditional end-of-season MotoGP test in Valencia on Nicky Hayden's championship-winning Honda RCV. It was an amazing reward for what I felt had been an extraordinary few years. From a motocross hopeful four years before, I'd taken some big steps to get this kind of invite from HRC. It would be not only an amazing experience but a chance to show Honda's Japanese bosses what I could really do.

That summer I was planning a move back to Northern Ireland where I wanted to buy a house. With some bonuses from Honda, Arai and Alpinestars for finishing fourth in the championship, plus some prize money from an off-season Sunflower Trophy I had ridden for Birdy in Northern Ireland, I was suddenly in a position to put down a deposit and become a property owner. I was still pretty young to be putting my foot on the first rung of the property ladder but, since I had left school after my GCSEs, I had felt that this kind of investment would stand me well for the future.

Then, still looking forward to the Valencia MotoGP test, I went back to Mallory Park for the Race of The Year and, during the warm-up, crashed and ruptured a cruciate ligament in my knee. I was so pissed off. It was painful and such a bitter pill to take. Instead of showing Honda bosses what I could do, I had to spend the next few weeks working on repairing the knee damage with Darren, hoping that a similar opportunity wasn't too far away.

All this time, lengthy conversations with Paul Denning and Colin Wright continued. Neil was offering about half what the other teams had put on the table: £40,000. But in the end the decision to stay with Honda was a no-brainer for me. I was able to take Chris Pike as my crew chief and work with a team I knew well; and I got an extra £2,000 to cover my travelling expenses from Northern Ireland. With my very first pay cheque from a motorcycle manufacturer, I was a professional Superbike rider at last.

I knew, though, that Kiyo was still Honda's number one rider, and I was always going to play second fiddle to him. I was still the young gun, just turned 20, while he was the favoured son of the Japanese factory who had won the championship the season before. That was part of the reason I had decided to leave Louth and move back to Northern Ireland to do my own thing.

That next season there were countless drives up and down the motorways to get home – the 4.15am sailing from Cairnryan to Larne became a true friend.

But it looked like it was going to be worth it. I started with a double podium at Brands Hatch and I was able to maintain a level of consistency throughout the season, not finishing outside the top five as we got to round six at Mondello Park in Ireland. I felt I was able to compete on equal terms with the big names, including my own team-mate. We were on the same equipment and, as any race fan knows, the first person you have to try to beat is your own team-mate. But I enjoyed some good battles with other top riders like Shane Byrne and his team-mate Tom Sykes, the Ducati pairing of Gregorio Lavilla and Leon Haslam and occasionally, in the second half of the season, Cal Crutchlow.

Mondello was my home race, about two hours' drive from where I was brought up, and loads of my family came down to stay together in a hotel called The Osprey to make a 'proper' weekend of it. The race was quite infamous for its Sunday night parties at a club called Time, which the whole paddock went to. And because the championship was predominantly confined to the UK mainland, the trip to Mondello was exciting for a lot of the teams and riders. It made them feel a bit more international by travelling across the water from Holyhead or Liverpool – it also made it a bit of a holiday race and always gave it a great atmosphere. It was a big deal for local fans too, because it was the highest-profile short-circuit race in Ireland.

Mondello is a very bumpy, narrow, tight and twisty track with no real straights, which makes it less than ideal as a circuit to let a 225bhp Superbike off the leash, so the two races were always going to be about managing the throttle and the grip levels.

My 2007 results were so much better and I was now a professional racer, so I was really nervous leading into the weekend and felt the pressure of expectation, not only from my family but from local media as well. All the talk and coverage was about 'when' I was going to win my first British Superbike race and not 'if'. Practice went OK, and I was in the top three in every session, but Superpole was really, really wet. I felt comfortable and confident going into the session though and ended up fastest – my second pole at Mondello, but this one felt more difficult to achieve, even though I was ahead of my team-mate, Kiyonari, on the other official Honda.

Race day was dry and, in race one, Leon Haslam grabbed the holeshot on his Ducati and I slotted in behind him for the first few laps, maintaining the gap at around 0.5s. At just over half race distance, on around lap 10, I started losing rear grip and there was nothing I could do to keep in touch. I got passed by Shakey Byrne and Greg Lavilla and was bitterly disappointed to finish fourth, almost 10 seconds behind Leon, who won the race.

We needed to make some changes to the bike for race two that would allow me to preserve some tyre for the latter stages of the race and maybe give myself a chance to get that first victory. I certainly felt confident enough, as long as my rear Michelin would last for the full 18 laps.

I got the holeshot in race two and, although Leon tried riding round the outside of me at the first turn, I held the tighter line which set me up nicely for the left-hander at turn two. I edged into a 0.5s lead but Leon was chasing hard and he had Shakey on his tail, who managed to get past both of us and into the lead on lap five. Kiyonari wanted some of the action too and, for the next couple of laps, the four of us were dicing for the podium positions. By lap 10 though, Shakey and I had broken clear and built a gap of 2.5s to Leon in third.

With just a tenth or two between me and Shakey, it looked like it would boil down to a straight duel between us. By about half race distance, he had built up a lead of about three-quarters of a second, but I felt comfortable because I was managing my rear tyre better. As the laps clicked by, I began to reel him back in and was feeling confident that I could manage the grip level until the end of the race. But I still had to pass him.

On lap 10, I took about three-tenths out of his lead and did the same on the next. Now I was right on his tail, but I'd been watching where I was a bit quicker than him and where I might be able to make a pass. I threw him a bit of a dummy on lap 13 around the left kink on the back straight and Shakey cut back underneath me as we went into the first part of the double right-hander at the bottom of the hill. But I knew that I was fast into the final corner, a tight right-hander that led back onto the start-finish straight. As we went through the fast left that precedes it, I got a really good drive and passed him going into the last corner.

I'd been able to save enough tyre for the end of the race and within about three corners I had opened up a gap of around half a second. I actually had enough rear grip to put in the fastest lap of the race on lap 16 and two laps later I crossed the line about 2.5s ahead of Shakey. I just felt relief more than anything – it was huge. It had been such a long time coming, and the expectations from so many people during that 2007 season were so high because I'd had a couple of podiums the year before, so I'd really been feeling the pressure. I was just screaming into my helmet all the way round the slow-down lap, until I met my mum and Uncle Barry at turn five. Uncle Barry had kept me going for a few years in the beginning with £5,000 in sponsorship, which was a heap of money for me and meant a hell of a lot.

On the track that day, he tied a Northern Ireland flag around my shoulders, which might not have been the most popular moment of the day with the local Dublin crowd, but we were all just a bit lost in the moment. My brain was going at 200mph and there was no conversation really, we all just screamed at each other. Then there was a cruise back to parc fermé with my visor open, taking in the reaction from the crowd and the congratulations from my fellow competitors – it was the most incredible couple of minutes that I wanted to last forever.

I screamed again as I climbed on to the top step of the podium for the first time since my motocross days, and I just took in a massive deep breath to savour the moment. I was a Superbike race winner for the first time; I sprayed the podium champagne like I really meant it, and the party that night in Time was off the scale.

That year I won four more races and finished on the podium a total of 16 times, which gave me the runner-up position in the championship behind Kiyo – an amazing 1–2 finish for Honda. I felt proud of what we achieved as a team and justified in my decision to stay for 2007. Their faith in me had been well placed. But I also felt this was just the start of bigger and better things.

It was a great season of firsts: I also rode for the first time in Japan, an audition test for the Suzuka 8 Hours. The Suzuka 8 is the most prestigious race for the Japanese factories, held at Honda's own circuit. It's part of the Endurance World Championship but it's the one all the manufacturers want to win and now, as an official BSB rider, I was being invited by Honda to their test in Japan. Some of the best Grand Prix and World Superbike riders have taken part and there are some pretty serious hoops you have to jump through to get selected.

I've been to Japan countless times since, but this was my first visit. Everything was new and different – food, cars, buildings, language. Apart from some tests in Spain, I hadn't really travelled outside the UK and it was an ordeal just getting there in the first place.

There were four places up for grabs in two separate two-man teams. Among the field was James Toseland, at the time leading the World Superbike Championship but rumoured to be joining a satellite Yamaha team in MotoGP the next season. There was Ryuichi Kiyonari, my team-mate in BSB and king of Suzuka after winning the race in 2005. Spanish Grand Prix rider Carlos Checa and former World Superbike and Japanese GP rider Tady Okada were also a worry. I was this kid from BSB suddenly fighting for a place in a full-on Honda team – an opportunity that could catapult my career in a completely new direction.

The audition test was pretty serious. I'd never had to try to hit a target average time over 28 laps before and I have never been so nervous as when I was getting changed before the race simulation.

I was used to tight and twisty BSB circuits, but this was a full-on F1 and MotoGP track: wide and fast with huge grandstands. My brain was getting overloaded with so much new information.

I went out and rode the very best I could. I was faster than James, faster than Checa – in fact, the only rider faster than me was Kiyonari, by 0.2s.

Then came the big announcement. The first team line-up was going to be Toseland and Kiyonari. The second team was going to be Checa and Okada.

I went quietly mental. I respectfully told the Honda management that I was really disappointed, then ran up to my tyre technician Daniel Croispine's office, where I checked his notebook for the proof: I was as fast as I thought.

Fuming, I got up to run back to the HRC office. Daniel grabbed me by the collar. 'There is a reason why you are not riding, Johnny,' he said. He was very calm. 'I don't know the reason, you will not be told the reason, and you do not need to know the reason. Just accept there is a reason, and there is no point getting angry about it because it will not change anything, OK?'

It was political. They had to choose the Japanese riders, and it seemed like Toseland had to be picked as a last attempt to persuade him to stay with Honda.

It didn't work out well for them though. Rather than the Suzuka 8 Hours, it became Toseland's infamous Suzuka eight minutes because he crashed after four laps. It was a real shame for everyone because his pace with Kiyonari was quite strong, but the race was eventually won by Suzuki.

For me, it was another missed chance. If I had raced, it could have been my way to show Honda's bosses in Japan what I was capable of. Maybe it would have led directly to a ride in World Superbikes the following year, or maybe even a route into MotoGP. Who knows?

What I knew for certain was that I had to make the step up to World Superbikes. If British Superbikes was the equivalent of the English Premier League, then WSBK was the Champions League and the World Cup rolled into one. It's where I wanted to be, where I stood the best chance of becoming a world champion. And it was clear I was going to have to make my own way there.

CHAPTER 7

LIVING THE DREAM

I WAS IN my third year of BSB, but I'd only ever seen it as a stepping stone. So, not long after that Suzuka 8 Hours disappointment in 2007, feeling Honda wasn't going to open many doors for me, I went to the World Superbike round at Brands Hatch to explore my options for making the step up the following season. James Toseland's manager Roger Burnett set up a meeting with Davide Tardozzi of Ducati to talk about me maybe riding with them alongside Troy Bayliss, already a double World Superbike champion. We had a good discussion and he seemed quite interested, as they were after a British rider to help with their Xerox sponsorship.

One issue I had was that the knee I'd injured at the Race of the Year at Mallory Park was still giving me a lot of problems and needed an operation, which I had scheduled for the end of the season. Roger said he had told Ducati all about it and everything was fine.

Until that point, I'd always managed my own contracts and negotiations, but I had been happy to work with Roger because he had set me up with a personal sponsorship deal through one of his business contacts the year before.

I also had a meeting with the Dutch Ten Kate official Honda team that Toseland was riding for. It was a well-sponsored, four-rider outfit, one of the biggest squads in the paddock, with two bikes in the World Superbike Championship and two in one of its support series, World Supersport. It was run by Gerrit ten Kate and his cousin Ronald, who had a Honda dealership and tuning shop in the Netherlands.

But Roger was not flavour of the month with the Ten Kate guys. Rider managers are never that popular and they knew Roger was working on taking Toseland to Yamaha in MotoGP. So, I met Gerrit and Ronald and Honda's Carlo Fiorani on my own. They confirmed Toseland was leaving and told me Honda wanted to bring Carlos Checa over from MotoGP. They were also looking at Ryuichi Kiyonari and Kenan Sofuoglu. Four riders don't fit on two bikes, so there clearly wasn't a ride for me.

They were pitching that I should ride in the World Supersport Championship instead and were trying to sell me on how great this would be for my career. After about five minutes I stood up and said, 'Thank you for the meeting but I'm only interested in a World Superbike ride.' I said goodbye and left.

Maybe that sounds a bit arrogant, but I had some bad memories of British Supersport with the broken femur, and at that point in the season I was running second in the BSB Championship, with four wins to my name, plus six or seven other podium finishes and a number of pole positions and fastest laps results, all against top-level riders including Kiyonari.

An hour later, Ronald rang to ask if I was still at the circuit, as they wanted a follow-up. They offered me a six-figure, three-year contract – the first year in Supersport followed by an option for years two and three in Superbike.

I knew how important the World Supersport Championship was to Honda in terms of bike sales and I was aware of just how much support went into the Ten Kate team, which had resulted in them winning the championship for the previous five consecutive seasons. But I was still reluctant. I thanked the guys again and said I'd think about it.

Two weeks later, I met with Roger again at the Cadwell Park round and we talked it over. I'd never had any clear answers about the details of this Ducati option, but we decided it was the most attractive. So, on the Sunday evening I climbed to the top of the hill at Cadwell to get a mobile signal and called Tardozzi. I was talking positively about the move and he was very warm to the idea and getting dead excited … until I mentioned this knee operation I needed. He sounded a bit confused. When I explained again, his mood turned quickly. He stopped talking about a factory ride and said they could consider, maybe, placing me in the Sterilgarda team, a Ducati satellite operation.

I politely thanked Tardozzi and said to Roger that I was going with Dad to Amsterdam the next morning to get a feel for the Ten Kate operation.

Ronald and Gerrit took me round their truly impressive dealership and race team workshop and I was starting to feel a bit special with these guys. It was a massive building with a very smart Honda dealership at the front, lots of shiny new Hondas with a big clothing and accessories show-room upstairs. The race team department was like a massive aircraft hangar with the four trucks just in front of the workshops. It was so clean you could eat your dinner off the floor.

They really treated Supersport seriously, built incredible bikes and the walls were lined with photographs of their world champions and some of their trophies. They were this close-knit family-run team and they spoke good English. At the end of the day I turned to Dad and said, 'I feel really wanted here. I want to do this.'

With Ducati forgotten, my only other attractive option was staying with Honda in BSB. Neil Tuxworth was pushing this hard, arguing he could help me more than Ten Kate because of his closer links to HRC. But not being selected for the Suzuka 8 Hours team had put a bit of a dampener on the whole HRC thing for me. There are no guarantees in racing, just a hell of a lot of politics.

So I rang Roger on the way back to Schiphol airport and told him the Ten Kate offer was right for me. He said, 'Well, I hope it goes well for you, but you're making the biggest mistake of your career.' That was certainly an opinion, but I wasn't bothered, I had a three-year contract at world championship level.

I like to be honest with people and the Ducati incident is one of the reasons I still like to be involved with all sporting and commercial offers that come my way.

To say I was excited wouldn't begin to describe it, and I went back to the British Superbike Championship with renewed inspiration and motivation. In the final round at Brands Hatch in mid-October, I took two second places to confirm my runner-up spot in the series. Another nice end-of-season bonus and a good way to bow out, with Kiyo winning the title and Honda taking a 1–2 finish.

My new contract with Ten Kate kicked in at the beginning of December and I had to get ready for a massive shift in lifestyle. I was having to think about getting visas, booking flights and hire cars – this was beyond Mum and Dad now. There was also the small matter of having to learn a load of new international circuits. Honda had a really good plan for this. They got me and my new team-mate, Andrew Pitt, on a press launch of the new 2008 Fireblade, at the Losail circuit in Qatar, the venue of the first round of the championship, and I got to do a lot of laps there.

At a party to mark the end of the launch, I had a stroke of luck when I got chatting to a race co-ordinator I knew called Tatia Weston. When I say, 'got chatting to' I mean 'shared a 2.00am, tequila-fuelled snog in the hotel pool with'. And when I say 'race co-ordinator' I mean 'absolute life saver' when it came to getting me around the world.

At the start of the launch, I had found out she'd arranged for me to have a Range Rover Sport as my hire car for the week. It was being used for the journalists' tracking shots, but I didn't care about that – I was 20 years old and thought it was pretty damn cool! Honda were lavish with their launches back then – honestly, no expense spared – and we were all staying in the Ritz Carlton. At the end of the week, after all the journalists had gone home, the events team were letting their hair down and I remember we were in a bar with a load of tequila shots lined up and I was lighting them before we knocked them back. So Tatia and I had that kiss and although nothing else happened that night, we swapped numbers and became pretty good friends.

We actually first met in the British Superbike paddock when I was in another relationship and our paths there crossed many times. She once drove me to Heathrow because I was going to Japan for the Suzuka 8 Hours test. We were laughing and joking in the car and I thought she was pretty cool. It was clear from the off that we had quite a flirty relationship and at the end of 2007 there was a Honda team event at the Sports Café in London. Tatia got a bit tired and emotional and I ended up putting her to bed, but I was actually a thorough gentleman that night.

She came in super-handy when things changed and I had to get organised. I was used to racing motorcycles – that was almost the easy part – but now I had to sort out flights, hire cars and other logistical issues. You can't forget your boots or helmet and have them sent next-day delivery to the other side of the world. It was as much a lesson in life as it was in sport, and Tatia knew her way around these things so she became my go-to girl that year for trains, planes and automobiles. If I needed a hire car somewhere or some advice on getting from an airport to a track, it was a phone call to Tatia to sort it all out.

She already had world championship experience with the Castrol Honda WSBK team and Honda's Formula 1 team and that year she was starting work with Paul Bird's VK Honda World Superbike team. I gave her my card details and she sometimes booked stuff for me, but it was all pretty cool because she was a mate, and whenever there was a post-race celebratory drink – and the paddock in 2008 was a great party venue on Sunday nights – we would always gravitate towards each other. We were both occasionally dating other people, but we couldn't stay away from each other if we had a few drinks.

However, she did sometimes find it quite difficult being Paul Bird's team co-ordinator and occasionally doing the walk of shame, sneaking out of my motorhome on a Monday morning.

To make the transition to the world championship easier, I also asked along one of my closest friends, Gary 'Gaz' Price, who I'd met through motocross. We'd hung out a lot in my last year in BSB and he was like my wingman, so he came to quite a few races. But he was useless when it came to logistics – he can't even find a way to pour himself a bowl of cereal for breakfast. Thank goodness for Tatia.

Getting my motorhome around Europe was also a new headache and I turned to a guy called Kevin Havenhand who had been working in the HM Plant Honda hospitality in BSB after he'd come back from the army. I asked if he wanted to drive my motorhome and he quickly said he'd do it for free if I paid his expenses. He got bored with doing it for free pretty quickly, but later we found him a job in the Ten Kate team hospitality and he's still working with me today as my assistant. Kev came along for the ride in 2008 and me, him and Gaz were ready, so we set off on this new adventure.

I went to a private pre-season test at Phillip Island in Australia – just the Supersport part of the team, because the new World Superbike race machines based on Honda's new CBR1000RR Fireblade that were being prepared by the team weren't yet ready. But the team took World Supersport seriously enough to pay for a test on the other side of the world and it really made me feel comfortable that I'd made the right decision.

Yamaha were at the Phillip Island test with Broc Parkes and Fabien Foret, which gave me a chance to evaluate the main opposition. I'd shed a few kilos over the winter and I had a great new team-mate in Andrew Pitt, who was a former World Supersport champion, but he'd won previously in World Superbikes, too. 'AP', as we call him, took his job very seriously but he was a great character to hang out with. He'd been around the block a bit, knew how the paddock worked and had a great sense of humour.

AP is a really intelligent guy – and a qualified accountant. He has a very dry sense of humour and is also very cultured, compared to what I was used to; he taught me you don't go to Pizza Hut to find a good pizza, you go to Bologna. He maintained a long-distance relationship with his Italian girl-friend Elisa and was a dedicated professional racer who took his training and nutrition very seriously. All in all, he was a great role model compared to some of my former team-mates.

I learned so much technically, too. Ronald asked AP and me to do side-by-side race simulations and AP and I brought back valuable data and worked incredibly well together. I would never dream of doing that with my team-mate today, but we had a special bond.

I immediately felt good on the bike and was fast straight away. I had a great team with crew chief Gigi, mechanic Michel, and Ronnie Schagen, a data engineer shared by me and Andrew. Ronnie taught me a hell of a lot about all the data a racing motorcycle can record, like suspension travel, degree of throttle opening, brake pressure, lean angles and the difference in speeds between the front and rear wheels. I could see what Andrew was doing on the bike, but Ronnie was able to show me how he was doing it and help me improve.

I'd only had five years of short-circuit racing, so there was still a huge learning process for me – new circuits, new techniques on the bike, new electronics with traction control. I had to adapt from riding the Superbike in BSB, on which you can brake later and then use its greater torque and horsepower to accelerate out of a corner.

I soaked up as much advice and data as possible and had as much fun as I could. Between sessions it was very light-hearted, and me and Gigi and Michel just used to rip the piss out of each other. We also got obsessed with TV shows like 24 with Kiefer Sutherland, and AP and I would watch back-to-back episodes in the motorhome and then go out on track and try to better each other's times in practice sessions or beat each other in the races.

I'd come from BSB where there was a lot of one-upmanship and quite a few people out to prove something every week. In the world championship paddock, it was much more relaxed. Nobody would rush home on a Sunday night, so there was a much better atmosphere. There was an understanding that once you got to that world championship level you were there for a good reason, you were there on merit. I really enjoyed being part of that paddock with people like Troy Bayliss, Troy Corser and other great champions.

There were other great characters like Nori Haga and Yukio Kagayama with their kids, plus real fun guys like Broc Parkes, Craig Jones and Peter Goddard from Öhlins. It was like a little travelling circus and every Sunday night we'd sink a few beers round each other's motorhomes. I remember being in our hospitality at Valencia in what turned out to be Bayliss's last season. He'd just dominated the first two Superbike rounds and he was smashed on beer and puffing on a cigarette. I was thinking, 'What's he doing? What's going on here?!' But he still won the title that year in style.

The first round was back at Losail in Qatar. The circuit is about 20km north of the capital Doha, in the middle of the desert. It's a flat and featureless track with no obvious landmarks but, because of its flowing nature, it's fun to ride once you've got your bearings and referenced your braking and turn-in points. It can be particularly tricky when the wind has been blowing because it will dump a load of desert sand on the track which makes it very slippery if you're a millimetre off the racing line.

I was confident I could be fighting near the front from the very first session. Practice went well but I had a big crash in qualifying – a rear-end slide coming out of the final corner – and was a little beaten up. There was only 20 minutes left in the session, so I hobbled back to the garage and went out on the spare bike. I pulled myself up from outside the top ten to fourth for a front-row start. AP had his own issues and had only managed 10th.

Race day was another warm day in Qatar, and although I was still a little sore I couldn't wait to get going. Fabien Foret blitzed the start from pole and I set off after him from the other end of the front row. By the time we got halfway round the opening lap, I was sat comfortably in second place.

And then ...

I was going through three fast rights, all third gear corners with each one a little bit slower and the last is probably 100mph or 160kph. Everything felt normal as I tipped in, but I entered the corner maybe a couple of kph too fast which took me just off the ideal line on to a sandy part. As I started to open the gas, the rear tyre let go without warning and then highsided me down the middle of the track.

Fuck! I've crashed in my first World Supersport race.

I landed really hard on my shoulder then was flipped over on to my stomach. As I slid down the track following my bike, AP had nowhere to go and crashed into my machine.

Fuck! I've screwed up my team-mate's race as well.

I had to dodge the other riders, who were still quite closely bunched as we were only on the opening lap. As the last guy went past me, I started to regain my breathing. My heart rate had gone through the roof and my hand was throbbing. My black and white glove was now a red glove and the end of one of the fingers had been worn away to just leave a bit of bone sticking out of the end.

I grabbed my wrist and held my hand up in the air. The back of my finger felt like it had exploded, it was virtually hanging off.

At the circuit medical centre, AP was sitting on the opposite side, absolutely devastated. There wasn't much conversation, and the looks I was getting from Elisa were pretty scary. However, although he had no points he also didn't have a scratch on him. She was acting like I'd completely wrecked his season.

Once everyone's sense of humour came back, the team joked that they'd never seen anyone highside a Supersport bike in third gear and it brought me the name 'Trigger Johnny' for a while.

My finger's never really recovered though.

A week later, I was able to ride with my hand heavily strapped in Australia. AP won the race, so all was forgiven pretty quickly, and I finished fifth and scored my first world championship points.

That fifth in Australia was followed by sixth at Valencia in Spain. Then I was all fired up when we got to the team's home race at the TT Circuit in Assen in the Netherlands, just 70km north of the Nieuwleusen workshop, and I took second, my first world championship podium. I was on the podium again at Misano at the end of June.

Then we went to Brno in the Czech Republic. During practice I had to spend a few laps figuring out which way it went and getting my braking markers clear in my head. It's a fast-flowing circuit that really suits an agile 600cc Supersport bike and by this time I had adapted my riding style to suit the higher corner speeds that Brno demands. I qualified seventh, but I got a great start and was third by the end of the first lap.

Unfortunately, I out-braked myself on lap four and had to fight my way back from sixth for a tight and exciting battle with AP and Craig Jones. Jonesy had a technical problem, so it came down to a straight fight between me and my team-mate, mentor and friend. I didn't let any of that emotional stuff get in the way though, and I beat him by about two-hundredths of a second. It was a 1–2 finish for the team and my first world championship victory. The champagne tasted so sweet.

I won in the following round at Brands Hatch and then again at Vallelunga in Italy. I remember that one particularly because, as I built quite a big lead, I started watching myself on these big video screens. I found the signal delay between what was being shown on the screens and what I was actually doing quite funny. As I was tipping into a corner, I was watching myself back-shifting a few seconds earlier. Everything seemed to be happening in slow motion. Looking back now, I realise I was really in the zone.

It's an incredibly personal feeling. Everything becomes automatic – all the repetition of braking, tipping in, apexing, accelerating. I stop thinking about racing, my mind can wander and I feel unstoppable, invincible, like nothing can go wrong. I am completely at one with the bike. When I'm in the zone, I'm so in tune with it I can sense the tiniest change in the level of grip or feel every slight ripple in the track surface. I haven't slowed, in fact the gap to the guy behind will continue to increase, but I feel almost still in time.

The next race was the penultimate round at Magny-Cours in France, and by then I had been on the podium in five successive races. The gap to AP was down to 11 points and I fancied my chances, but on race day another rider crashed going into the hairpin at the end of the long straight. He not only took me out of the race but the championship fight. AP won the race and took enough points for the title with one round remaining.

That night was hard to deal with. There was a big championship party, 'We Are The Champions' by Queen blasting out over and over again. But not for me.

It had been a pretty awesome year all the same – Honda Europe soon decided to stop paying bonuses in Supersport because Ten Kate riders were always winning!

What really topped it off was that Honda also said they were going to exercise their option on the contract and take me up to World Superbikes for 2009. So much for the 'biggest mistake of my career'.

Sadly, it meant AP would miss out, which made things a little awkward. I felt for him. He'd done everything right and he should have got the ride, too. He didn't say anything negative to me, or about me, but I watched him not exactly holding back in a heat-of-the-moment interview with

Charlie Hiscott on Eurosport. He suggested I'd been picked because of my passport, implying the championship needed a British rider, rather than another Australian. He was angry and I completely get that, but he was always fine with me.

For the final round in Portimao, Portugal, the team and I decided I should switch to the Superbike. Kenan Sofuoglu was quite keen to return to Supersport after a tough rookie year, so we just swapped bikes.

I qualified alongside Troy Bayliss on the front row – an amazing moment and, at the age of 21, I felt this mix of pride, excitement and nerves. But I didn't feel out of my depth. I had Superbike experience from the UK and almost a full season of world championship racing under my belt and I finished fourth.

Meanwhile, in World Supersport Josh Brookes, who had been lying third, didn't score enough points to overtake me, so I finished second in that championship. It was another nice little bonus cheque for me and a fantastic 1–2 for Honda and the team. There were no mixed emotions that night and, after I collected my FIM silver medal at the end-of-season awards, we had an absolutely huge party too.

When we got back to the paddock that night, my rental car came in for some serious abuse from some fairly senior members of the team. The next morning, as I surveyed the wreckage through the fog of a very bad hangover, I thought: 'This could be real. I could actually achieve my dream here and become a world champion.'

CHAPTER 8

MY RACER'S BRAIN

THAT FIRST YEAR of world championship racing was amazing, I was 21 and living the dream. But that season we had to endure a nightmare too.

I had got to know Craig Jones in 2005, when I'd just moved away from home and was living like a nomad. I spent a lot of time with Jonesy in his house in Peterborough when he and his girlfriend Karen took me under their wing. I really admired him and in those younger years I thought, if I managed to get from the sport all that he had, I would have succeeded. He had a lot of things I really aspired to back then: nice sporty car, mini-bikes, a beautiful house with Karen.

Jonesy was one of the biggest characters in the paddock, a popular joker who loved to talk a load of crap. He honestly could have sold snow to Eskimos, and it seemed he had it made because his life was so full of fun and he did everything with a massive smile on his face. While I lived with him, he signed a pretty big contract to ride for Carl Fogarty's Foggy Petronas team in World Superbikes. The bike wasn't at all competitive, but Jonesy didn't care, he just laughed because he was all about the money and extracting as much fun and enjoyment as he possibly could out of life. I learned a huge amount from him about not taking life too seriously and finding time to really enjoy opportunities when they come your way.

After his World Superbike adventure, Jonesy came back to World Supersport in 2008 on a competitive Honda and we were big rivals, but still good friends. Between Misano, where he and I shared a special moment on the podium with AP, and that amazing battle for my first race win at Brno, we spent a couple of weeks touring around various European campsites in our motorhomes. It was truly magical. In Riccione, near the Misano circuit, Jonesy and my mate Gaz took a scooter out to find some pizza one night and managed to tuck the front and crashed at a little sandy roundabout, which caused some mayhem. Broc Parkes, who was a good party animal, was also with us at that point and he'd won at Misano, so we all made a lot of noise and got on with what a bunch of lads would do in a campsite bar. Broc didn't get on so well with one of the security guards though and eventually we got asked to leave the campsite.

The following week, we found an amazing campsite in southern Austria on our way up to the Czech Republic. It bordered on to a beautiful lake and had a load of water flumes or slides, so we'd have fun there like a bunch of kids during the day and rent some bikes to ride round the lake, and then cook a barbeque at our motorhomes in the evening before jumping back into the lake.

Having laughed almost non-stop for those weeks, we came back for the next race at Brands Hatch. On the Saturday night before the race, Jonesy and I bumped into each other on our scooters in the paddock. The race was always going to come down to making the right tyre choice, and when he told me he was going with the softer race tyre I remember thinking it was a bit of a gamble. On race day, I'd qualified on pole position and asked one of my mechanics to go and check which tyre Craig had on. Needless to say, it was the exact opposite of the one he told me he was going to use!

It was a typical Jonesy, Jack-the-lad, jokey kind of thing and, just like at Brno in the previous round, we ended up having a massive bar-to-bar battle in the race with Andrew Pitt. I remember thinking if the rest of the season was going to be like this, it was going to be one hell of a spectacle. It was warm but overcast, and the rain had held off for our race. From pole position, I'd managed to get to the front and was just focused on staying ahead of Jonesy and AP, but after about ten laps it started to rain and the red flags came out to stop the race. Although World Supersport bikes run treaded tyres, they're still very slippery when it's raining, and race control decided it was too dangerous to continue. The race was restarted with the result to be declared on aggregate times of the two parts, but the red flags came out again after another five or six laps.

I assumed there had been a crash or that there was some oil down on the circuit somewhere and, in my racer's brain, I was immediately annoyed that I might have had another potential win taken from me.

I didn't know what had happened until I got back to the garage. At the end of lap 16, Jonesy had crashed behind me coming out of Clearways, the final fast corner at Brands. As crashes go, it shouldn't have been too bad, but he was hit by another bike and knocked unconscious, so the race was stopped. Some guys in the team had seen it on the TV monitors and said it looked pretty bad.

To this day I haven't watched the crash. I never want to dwell on the details. I can remember Gaz and I just hanging around all evening waiting for Karen to give us some news. Eventually, my team took me aside. Jonesy had succumbed to his injuries.

I just went numb. We had spent the previous few weeks having the best fun a couple of lads could have, and now he wasn't there. None of it made any sense. This dream shouldn't be ending like this.

That evening as everyone packed away the awning and equipment, it was very quiet. There were a lot of people looking vacant, lost in their own thoughts at the enormity of what had happened and the realisation that Jonesy wouldn't be coming back.

Although it was meaningless to everyone at the time, the result was declared later with the positions that we were in before the accident and I ended up with 25 points, with Jonesy in second and AP third. What I would have given to have shared that podium with him too, at our home race in front of an enthusiastic British crowd. But there was no podium that day.

I really miss Jonesy and still think about him heaps, and I'll always be grateful to him and Karen for looking after me in 2005.

His death was particularly close to home, but it wasn't my first encounter with the very worst aspect of motorcycle racing. We all know how dangerous our profession is, and on the back of every disclaimer you sign it's written in big, bold letters: 'Motorsport is dangerous.' Of course, a lot of different factors go into making it as safe as possible and, as well as the advanced protective gear we wear – helmet, leathers, back and chest protectors, boots, gloves – the circuits are generally safe, too. Highside crashes are never nice, because when you're thrown into the air you fall onto tarmac from height and at speed, so it's going to hurt. But a front-end crash, when your front tyre loses grip, usually results in a slide into a gravel trap and you can often pick yourself up and dust yourself down to have another go. But when you're in close proximity to other bikes, like Jonesy was, the results can be much worse. Nearly all the bad crashes on short circuits in recent years have been the result of a rider being hit by another bike.

I'd been close to the young Red Bull Rookie rider Chris Jones, no relation to Craig, who was only 14 when he died in a start line crash at Cadwell Park in 2005.

I was in my first year of British Superbikes and we had both spent the week before the race staying in Louth, train-ing together and just hanging out. I learned that he was a really lovely kid. The day itself was dry and sunny. The 125 race was on before us and as they completed their warm-up lap and reformed on the grid, I was keeping my eye on the lights to get an idea how the starter was working them that day.

Chris had qualified well in fourth and was on the far side of the front row of the grid, just in front of the big crowd that usually gathers on the grassy slope alongside the Cadwell start-finish straight. As I stood at the side of the track for the start of his race, the red lights came on and went off again a few seconds later to signal the start. The air was filled with the howl of about 30 two-stroke machines and I immediately looked across at Chris to watch his geta-way, but he had stalled.

I could hardly hear myself with the sound of the bikes, but I was screaming, terrified he was going to get hit by a rider coming from behind. Then, like in slow-motion, the impact came. It was horrible. I waited in shock in the stunned silence, unable to speak, desperate to see Chris get up or move his limbs. But nothing happened. He didn't move.

Chris's death was a huge blow because he was so young with a lot of life left to live, but I'm so glad I got to see his personal side in that week before the race.

We knew each other in the paddock but had never really got a chance to hang out, even though we were in the same team set-up. I remember I had a little Peugeot 206 at the time and took it up to the team's workshop to hoover it out and clean it. Chris was with me and we just spent the time talking about music and the kinds of things young lads talk about. He was just getting into girls, so we shared some experiences, and he really came out of his shell because he was usually with his family at race meetings and we never had an opportunity to talk.

He died doing what he loved and, while his life was very short, it was incredibly full. The toughest part for me is that nobody ever got to see how good he was going to be, and I guess that's the racer's brain talking because he was such a naturally gifted racer. The human side of it all never really touched me until I went to the funeral where I saw that he was a brother, a son, a grandson, a cousin, a nephew, and it was then that I realised that this wasn't just a massive loss for our sport.

But on the day he died, even though it was unbelievably tough to witness his accident, I knew I had to separate what happened from what I was doing myself just an hour or so later. And I did, I was able to delay processing it until later and it felt very matter-of-fact in my brain.

Perhaps I can be so matter-of-fact about deaths and injury because of the pure road-racing environment I grew up in with Dad. We can watch a video of him racing back in the day and a good chunk of the grid are no longer here. He always counts himself very lucky that he got out of the game intact.

I'VE CRASHED AND crashed and always got back on the bike as soon as I could, ever since that Christmas when I first started riding the little Italjet. Even back then, there was never an 'Ouch, I've hurt my knee', or even a worry that it was going to happen again; as the years went by and the injury list grew, it was just a question of dealing with the pain, or parking any emotion attached to it, and getting back on.

When I have injuries, I feel this huge motivation to come back stronger. I'm at my absolute best on the track and in my training when I'm on the mend. My life never has more structure than it does at these times – it's a rigid routine of physiotherapy, hyperbaric chambers, rehabilitation. I like to stay away from the track during the whole process and that absence makes me more motivated to work and come back stronger.

Before every weekend I'll be anxious, but it'll be about race-related things, whether I'll find that special relationship I'm looking for with the bike. And after the first couple of sessions, those nerves usually go away. As I head towards the race, I'll be nervous about not getting a good start or whether we've made the right tyre choice. Strangely, any nerves are often helped by my kids, who have allowed me to detach myself from those kind of obsessions. Sometimes, when you're trying to solve a particular issue, you can end up creating more problems and getting further away from any kind of solution; when you become desperate to find a way forward you often get more lost.

I can be with my family right up until the final moments. It's almost like I have two completely different personalities – a normal, down-to-earth guy right up until that moment I pull on the helmet when I turn into the racer.

I love that they come to all the races. The working me – withdrawn, focused, intense – is very different to the 'domestic' me, who loves to cook and be a hands-on dad. I go in minutes from a comfortable armchair in my motorhome to the seat of a 200mph rocket. Off the track, I'm a mellow family guy. The moment the visor comes down, I'm a Marvel movie superhero.

On the track, I'm one of the most aggressive guys out there, to the extent that, when they introduced a new World Superbike regulation a couple of years ago to reverse the front part of the grid to make the second race more exciting, I kind of made a joke of it because often, starting from the back of the third row, I'd be near the front after the first lap.

I'm tunnel-visioned and very selfish. If it was about enjoyment, I'd be riding my motocross bike. If I was just out to have some fun, I'd be on a track with my two young kids or my brothers and friends, so we could all enjoy it. But my job is about winning and winning at a world level, and that's the way I treat it. Of course, I try to enjoy it along the way and having the family around helps me a lot and helps to channel my emotions over a weekend, but it's really geared towards me trying to go out there and get a result.

Sometimes, I get to see it from the outside when I go and visit races in MotoGP or British Superbike. I often think that a rider could be a lot faster if he'd just relax and loosen up a bit, but I'd never tell them how to do their thing because it's so personal. I know riders who just obsess about their sport and can't sleep before a race because they're so wound up and nervous. Others live within the confines of the gym, smashing themselves to bits, week in, week out. I seem to have found a balance now. I can honestly say that nine times out of ten I'll leave the garage after a session or at the end of the day and not stress too much about what's going on with the bike on track. Of course, there are times when your emotions can get the better of you and that inner chimp is dominating you a little bit more than you'd like, but that's why I really enjoy the family being there. In those moments, I can't let them know how stressed I am, but I can take the boys for a run on their bikes in the paddock just to get away and detach myself for a few minutes. When they're not there, I have more time on my hands to stress. The race weekend schedule has become so packed with post-session debriefs and media commitments that I really enjoy getting back to the motorhome for a cup of tea with the family whenever I can because they're always there for me.

I sleep like a baby before races because I've learned not to worry about things I can't control, but to focus instead on doing the best that I can with the settings we've got on the bike. That's been a massive learning process over the years. I spent time working with sports psychologists when I was with Red Bull, when I often worried about things that I couldn't control during a race. 'What if I get a bad start?' 'What if I can't cut through the traffic quickly enough?' 'What if I get held up behind this slower rider?' 'What if the tyre I've chosen isn't right?' It taught me how to focus on positive thoughts, targeting the things I can control and concentrating on doing them as well as possible. It's definitely something that I've developed during my career, because when I was doing schoolboy motocross I was one of those kids who would crash twice on one lap and still try to win. Now I feel like a much more rounded person – not so edgy or 'mood-swingy'. I have a 'what will be, will be' attitude and my approach now is just to go out on the day and do the best I can with what I've got.

Sometimes, in a weird kind of way, the detachment I feel on a race weekend can also take the edge off winning. The sheer euphoria of victory, screaming in my helmet with that incredible buzz of joy and relief when I'm the first rider to see the chequered flag, is truly amazing, but it often wears off a bit as I make my way round the slow-down lap. Then I get back to parc fermé and see the team and my family waiting for me and I feed off how super-happy they are and in those moments the feeling comes back. The coolest part about doing this with my family by my side, plus Kev, my assistant, who has become one of the people closest to me, is that we all get to savour the moment and enjoy a few celebratory drinks together in the paddock on a Sunday night after a good weekend.

After that, for me, it's pretty much on to the next one.

CHAPTER 9

THE LEARNING CURVE

TOWARDS THE END of 2008, I got some shocking family news. Mum called and said she and Dad were separating and she wouldn't be at home when I got back from the final race of the season. She said she'd not been happy for a long time, that she'd had enough of my dad and wanted to go her own way. I think she'd been building up to the decision for a while, maybe years, but when she decided that it was time to move on she delayed telling us until after my first world championship season was over.

I was grateful for that but the news still knocked me sideways. The tight family unit I'd grown up in was breaking apart. It was a period that was tough on everyone, especially on my younger brother and sister. They were barely scratching their teens and weren't really old enough to understand what was happening. I was aware my parents' relationship wasn't perfect, and I had often heard arguments late at night about the general stresses and strains of bringing up four children. I was old enough by then to realise it would be selfish to want them to stay together when they didn't want to.

I actually had this feeling that both my parents had failed. I didn't want to talk about their relationship or be involved in it, because I didn't have the greatest sympathy for either of them. I knew they'd both played their part in the break-up. Dad liked a drink now and again, and when he'd had a couple his character could change a bit. I guess what his shyness usually kept covered would come out. On the other side of that, Mum's clever enough and knows how to push people's buttons to get a reaction.

The atmosphere at home made me feel very uncomfortable and I could only think about getting away, which I was then in a position to do. Kristofer and Chloe were much younger and I really felt for them, because I think you need that balanced parenting when you're growing up. I felt especially bad for Chloe, because she was so young and the age gap between us meant we never really hung out together. She's so cool now though, and she's turned out great. I follow her student world on Instagram and she's a proper little socialite. I know that if I was her age, I'd want to hang out with her!

Kristofer suffered particularly because in the early days he decided that he wanted to spend his time equally between Mum and Dad, spending a week with her and the following week with him. I think it probably messed with his head and he ended up spending a lot of his time on the McCammonds' farm. Good old Philip and his family came to the rescue again. It all combined to make me feel guilty, because neither Kristofer nor Chloe got to enjoy that solid and happy family environment throughout their childhood like I had.

But it was Richard, closest to me in age, who probably bore the biggest brunt. There wasn't much room for him in the tiny cottage Mum found to rent. It was a new start for her and it was close to her sister, so I think she saw it as a little haven for her and Chloe. Her landlords were really kind to her and she was happy enough there but, while we were always welcome, it was a bit of a squeeze and Richard spent most of his time with Dad. He was also working in the family business by then, but he couldn't wait to get away. As soon as he was able, at 19, he scraped enough together for a deposit, got himself a mortgage and moved out.

I admire him so much for how he dealt with the whole situation. He is so kind-hearted and tries to keep everyone happy. He usually succeeds, too. There was a year or two when he was my only contact at home, the one I'd check in with to find out how everyone was and what was happening. And I'm so grateful he never let on how bad things really were for them all. He kept a lot from me because he always had my best interests at heart, and he still does.

After she moved out of the family home, Mum stopped working with Dad and lost the wages she'd been earning from Rea Distribution. To her credit, she got a part-time job with the local education board and topped up her income by working in a supermarket. When the education-board job became full time and permanent, Mum got the role. She settled into her cosy little country cottage and started to get her life back on course. Eventually, though, Mum and Chloe moved into the house I'd bought in Larne.

I'm not sure either Mum or Dad were that much happier after separating, but I think it was a lot simpler for him as he's not such a complex character and he was able to find someone after a while, so he got back to motoring along happily enough. Mum had to work a little harder than Dad to get back on track, but I'm so proud of the way she's achieved that. She was always the solid foundation that the family was built on, but since we've had kids she's become a rock of continual support for Tatia and me and she's the most fantastic grandmother for our boys.

AMID ALL THE family issues, I was longing for the 2009 season to start. It felt like my moment had finally come. I was lining up alongside Carlos Checa in the main Hannspree Honda World Superbike team, with Ryuichi Kiyonari in the same garage but racing under different colours.

I was relishing the opportunity, but there was still a lot of learning to be done, along a very steep curve. The bike was so different from my last Superbike experience in the British championship two years before; in fact, the Ten Kate bike was more like the light switch machine I'd first ridden in Red Bull colours four years earlier. The new model had been launched by Honda in 2008, but the race bike was a 230hp monster, and apart from a couple of wins with Checa and Kiyonari, its results hadn't been great. Ten Kate was a tuning company and they always wanted to see huge power curves and crazy horsepower figures, but strangely that doesn't always translate into a bike that can give you a fast lap time.

Sometimes you need a bike that's smooth and easy to ride to make a quick lap.

The CBR's problems were highlighted during testing and when the new season finally got underway, first in Australia and then Qatar, I found it so difficult to ride I ended up falling out with Ronald. My crew chief William Huistjes was technically very good, but only a couple of years older than me, so it was difficult to feel confident in his experience. I started with a couple of top tens in Australia, even though I qualified third and led the first couple of laps of the new season. But I just found it so difficult to maintain my pace. The bike didn't want to turn, handled like it wanted to spit me off all the time and I couldn't get the rear tyre to last because it was spinning up as I exited every corner.

Round two in Qatar, where I qualified 17th, was even worse but, when I tried to suggest what changes the bike might need to perform better, I was made to feel like I was the young, inexperienced guy in the team again – similar to the feelings I got from Havier Beltran in my first years in BSB. The management was just telling me to get on with it and ride the bike, but I knew it wasn't right. So, I started second guessing the team and was reaching out a lot to Chris Pike, my old crew chief from BSB, for some set-up advice. I knew I could do a good job and I believed in myself. I was the guy out there riding the thing on the track, feeling like I was just waiting for a crash and possible injury. I didn't know which way to turn and started to feel so low and demotivated that for the first and only time in my career, I found myself thinking about just walking away.

Around this time, Tatia and I started getting together a bit more, even though we each technically had other partners and she was trying to put up barriers to stop anything getting more serious between us. I thought it would be amazing to get together properly but, as much as she was wanting me to lay my cards on the table, I think she was a little mortified about the feelings she had for me and the fact that she might be falling for me. She kept putting up defences and saying things like, 'Listen, I'm not your girlfriend, right?' and 'Stop trying to define what kind of relationship we have.' That might not have been the right thing to say to a 21-year-old world championship motorcycle racer who had the world at his feet and had 'opportunities' left, right and centre. I totally respected her feelings and I understood that she didn't want a permanent relationship – I wasn't expecting her to say, 'Let's get married, I'll look after you and have your kids.' For me that was fine, I had way too much life to live at that age – it was like being told to have your cake and eat it. So I ate a bit of cake every now and again, but it always came back to a Sunday night after a race. After a few drinks we'd gravitate towards each other again.

Meanwhile, the issues with the bike really came to a head in Valencia, a tight and twisty circuit with a lot of first and second gear corners that really showed up the problems. I felt like I was doing 10 rounds with Anthony Joshua every time I went out for a practice session. The discussions with the team got increasingly desperate.

Then Ronald said to me the night before the race that they'd start listening to me when they felt I was riding the bike to its full potential, which really pissed me off.

I crashed in race one and barely made it into the points in race two. It was getting worse. I couldn't face the usual technical debrief and went straight to my motorhome in tears. Ronald came in as I was unzipping one of my boots. I told him to get the fuck out of my motorhome and flicked the boot in the direction of his head. He followed my advice pretty quickly, otherwise he might have had an Alpinestars logo imprinted on his forehead.

I picked myself up and drove to the airport to fly home to Northern Ireland. It was Easter and there were some races the following weekend at Kirkistown and Bishopscourt where my good friend Keith Amor was riding. Keith is so positive and full of energy he could make anyone smile, whatever their mood. I told him, 'I just don't know what to do. I'm meant to be living the dream in the World Superbike Championship, but I'm not enjoying riding the bike and it's doing my fucking head in.' He was always on my side, but his attitude was just to keep plugging away and not to get too worked up. 'Don't take it so seriously,' he said. 'Look, let's just go out and get bent in half in Belfast to take your mind off it.'

So, with another good friend from motocross days, Neil 'Tubman' Thompson, we got absolutely hammered, to the extent I woke the following morning in Tubman's house in Antrim and Keith woke up at my house in Larne, 25 miles away. He didn't have any keys, so he broke in by popping open a front window. We'd been planning to go and watch some motocross that day but I was in no state to drive, so we asked our mate Sean if he'd drive my car to the track and give us a chance to catch up on a bit of shut-eye.

As we were driving, Ronald rang and was on the car's loudspeaker. There was me wanting to heave, trying to stop all my mates laughing and trying to have a sensible conversation with my team boss. I figured out he was saying the team really understood what I was going through and wanted to do a private test with me – no Checa or Kiyo. When could I be in Amsterdam? Fighting back my hangover, I told him I'd be there the next day, but he replied, 'No, we're testing tomorrow, you need to be there tonight.'

So, I got on the phone to Tatia. Could she get me to Amsterdam that night? I still had to get hold of my wingman, Keith, who'd left his passport in Tubman's house. We made it and luckily it wasn't a two-day hangover, because we started testing the following morning at an oval circuit called Lelystad, where the lap was precisely 14 seconds long. I must have done hundreds of laps, working on the fuelling and getting the team's engine tuner and electronics engineer to take power away from the engine. They couldn't believe I was asking for less power. Although I was tired and kind of dizzy, I came away from the test feeling the team was starting to listen and I was no longer being asked to ride a fire-breathing animal that wanted to kill me. The progress came mostly in the corner exit, which before was so difficult because of all the power being put through the rear tyre. Now that power was more controllable, the tyre gripped better and the bike went where I wanted it to. The team had taken a leap of faith in trusting my feelings and they'd seen the improvements.

Assen was our first chance to test the engine configuration on a real track and we got seventh and fifth, definitely moving in the right direction. I went five-four in Monza then scored my first World Superbike podium at Kyalami in South Africa. The sheer elation of spraying and tasting champagne again was combined with some relief and satisfaction.

While there, I had another bit of an encounter with Tatia. She is the life and soul of a party, especially if she's had a couple of drinks, and she ended up with half the paddock in a local bar on the Sunday night. It was actually her 30th birthday as well. I called her and asked if she wanted to come back to the team hotel where I was having a couple of beers with my crew. She said yes, so I went to get her, but by the time I got to the bar she was blind drunk. I thought the gentlemanly thing to do would be to ask my mechanic, who wasn't drinking at the time, if he would be kind enough to drive her back to her hotel. She was suffering the next day, but we managed to talk on the phone and I explained what had happened, so things were all fine.

Tatia was also pretty good friends with my mate Gaz, and one day soon after that he rang her and painted some quite colourful stories about me and other women, a lot of which were a bit exaggerated because she told me what he'd said. Gaz had spent most of the previous year travelling around the world with me, but we ended up having a bit of a fallout over this and I had to kick him off the team for a while.

BACK ON THE track, Kyalami was followed by another podium at Salt Lake City in the USA, by which stage I think the team was beginning to understand I was the real deal and not some young rookie who should do as he was told.

There was something else bothering me too: the suspension. The team had been using WP suspension for years and years, and while it worked great in Supersport, they had never really done much in Superbike. It was so stiff and strong I could have ridden the bike into a brick wall at 100mph and we could still have used the forks in the next race. Our rivals used Öhlins and I really wanted to try it. For a second time, they trusted my judgement and made an expensive decision to fix the shiny new gold-coloured suspension on my bike. Without any testing, we used it in the next round.

Misano is on the Italian Riviera on the Adriatic coast and it's always a favourite because the weather's great, the beach is nearby and the Italian fans are just so passionate about their racing. The circuit is about an hour down the road from the Ducati factory, so they never let you forget where you are and who they'd like to see winning – an Italian rider on an Italian bike at an Italian circuit.

Despite not having had a chance to dial in our new suspension, I qualified second fastest just behind a Ducati ridden by Czech rider Jakub Smrz. Ben Spies, who was lighting up the championship that year on a Yamaha, was third, with Italian Michel Fabrizio on the factory Ducati completing the front row. His team-mate, Noriyuki Haga, was sixth with my own team-mates Checa and Kiyonari alongside him on row two.

Race one started wet, which was really unfortunate because we'd had no chance to ride with the new suspension in those conditions. Apart from Spies, who won, it turned into a Ducati-fest with their bikes taking the other two podium places plus fourth and fifth as well. But race two was dry and I felt much more confident as the lights went out and we charged down to turn one. I was in a good position, but then Haga screamed down to take the holeshot while I scrapped a bit with Ben Spies for second. As the race settled down I was in second, shadowing Haga. I was conscious of looking after the rear tyre to make sure I had some grip left at the end.

Fabrizio had got up to third to form a kind of Ducati sandwich with me as the filling. I didn't fancy that too much and on lap four got in front of Haga for the lead. The two Ducatis were right on my tail, so there was no way I could afford to make the smallest mistake. Fabrizio got past his team-mate for second, but they ended up fighting each other a little, which allowed me to open a small gap where I stayed for the next 12 laps. But I couldn't get away and once they'd stopped scrapping they were able to reel me back a bit.

None of us knew it at the time, but Valentino Rossi, who lived just a few kilometres up the road in Tavullia, was watching the show we were putting on from the middle of the circuit.

Fabrizio passed me at the beginning of lap 17, but Haga, being the senior rider on identical machinery, was desperate not to let his team-mate beat him, so a couple of laps later he forced his way past to leave me third. But three corners later, I was back up to second and in turn one of the last lap I slipped past Fabrizio. He was desperate to take the place back and to be that Italian winner on the Italian bike at the Italian circuit, but I had enough tyre left to get a really good drive down the back straight and I held him off to take my first World Superbike win. I was delighted for the team, who had worked so hard to get the Öhlins suspension on the bike, and I felt so satisfied with my own performance. I was beginning to have an influence over the direction of the bike's development and my own career.

There was a perfect symmetry on the podium, with me on the top step and the red and white Ducati riders on either side. It was the best feeling ever, because it had been such a turnaround in the five rounds since the problems we had in Valencia. I felt I'd proved myself to be not only a world-class racer, but a rider who knew what was needed to make the bike work for me. We partied very hard that night, and from that point on I was a regular front runner.

Tatia and I also marked the start of our official relationship with that first World Superbike win. She must have taken Gaz's phone call quite seriously, because after it she had called me and said, 'Look, let's forget everything, you're obviously too busy doing what you're doing. You can't be what I want you to be because we're in different places and looking for different things.' I was like, 'Well, why don't you just give me a chance, instead of putting up this barrier all the time? Why don't we give it a go and see what happens?'

She was living in Cannes, in France, at the time, so I flew down there and we had a good chat. We went to Misano together and said, 'Right, let's do this!' It may have been the first sober time we'd slept together, because Tatia says she can't remember any of the earlier occasions.

After the race, we did a nice little road trip together back up to the UK for the next round a week later. As we were driving, some strange, off-track developments came to the surface. The team had a really weird sponsor, and it turned out they hadn't been paying their bills. It got to the point where Gerrit ten Kate, the team principal, was almost having to re-mortgage his house to keep the team going. It was affecting my finances, too, because I was owed €90,000 by the team. This outstanding amount hadn't eased my early season feelings of frustration and, although I was on a massive high after that debut victory, some doubts remained.

As we drove up through Italy and Germany, Yamaha's Maio Meregalli, who is now Valentino Rossi's team manager in MotoGP, called me. He was basically offering me a contract to ride an R1 in 2010, but the problem was I still had another year to see out with Honda. That said, I was owed ninety grand and Ben Spies was showing how competitive the Yamaha was, so I called Linda Pelham for some advice.

She put me in touch with a Formula 1 lawyer and I quickly sent him a copy of my agreement. He basically agreed that Ten Kate were in breach of contract and we could serve them with a notice of termination. Formula 1 lawyers don't come cheap though, and after a few meetings I had to pay £8,000 for the privilege of being told something I already knew. By this time, my discussions with Yamaha had gone up to head office and I was talking details with Laurens Kleinkoerkamp, racing boss of Yamaha Europe. He was asking for evidence that my team was in breach of contract, but these kinds of contracts are commercially very sensitive and confidential, so I was in a real catch-22 situation – they couldn't satisfy themselves I could get out of the contract unless I showed it to them, and I couldn't show it to them without breaching my contract.

I served the team with notice, demanding the settlement of all outstanding payments within 14 days, and 24 hours later there was €90,000 in my bank account from Honda. It was satisfying to finally get paid, even though it meant the Yamaha deal was out of reach.

That £8,000 bill from the lawyer got me thinking that perhaps I needed some professional advice in my business and financial affairs. Until that point, my parents had looked after things, but in the mess of their divorce, it was under-standable that their minds were on other things. Mum had a lot of other distractions, and the time was right for me to start looking at professional business management.

A guy called Chuck Aksland had been manager of Kenny Roberts' MotoGP team and he had a great reputation in the paddock. Chuck came to the World Superbike round in the UK after my win in Misano and explained his company, International Racers, looked after guys like Wayne Rainey, Kevin Schwantz and the Hayden brothers. These guys were all financially secure for life and that's what I was aiming for. The company have looked after my contract negotiations and endorsements, my business and investments ever since.

There was just the small matter of calling Mum to tell her about this decision. I had knots in my stomach, not really sure how she'd react. I started: 'Mum, I know you've looked after everything since the beginning, and you know how grateful I am, but I've got to a point now where I need some professional management people to look after me.' There was a long pause. 'What are you saying?' she said in a slightly broken voice. I explained I needed people who understood the world championship paddock and knew how it worked. I could hear her weeping a bit. I explained I needed people to negotiate on my behalf, to look after my banking and finances. And I said I needed to be able to roast those people if I didn't think they were doing a good job. 'I'd never be able to do that with you,' I said, 'and I just want you to become my mum again.'

She just carried on crying. I think she felt I was abandoning her, which upset me as well. I totally wasn't – I knew what an amazing job she'd done for me up to that point and how much she had supported everything in my career. I just wanted to go back to the mother-and-son relationship with no business complications, but maybe I didn't explain my feelings or motives very well because the whole saga put a bit of pressure on our relationship for a good while.

It was the right thing to do though. I wanted to stand on my own two feet. It was something I was already doing better, as I developed my own confidence in trusting my instincts and judgement.

The conversations with Yamaha had no negative effect on my relationship with the team, and my renewed confidence in the bike led me to win another race later that season at the Nürburgring in Germany, beating Ben Spies and setting a lap record on the last lap that stood for a few years.

The team were believing in me, and I was earning their respect. I could see them thinking maybe they needed to change their philosophy a little bit. They were used to building bikes whose engines were so powerful they sometimes made the rider look better than they really were. So while there was no doubt they could build a fast bike, the team had some pretty stiff competition in 2009: Yamaha had come with a new line-up of Ben Spies and Tom Sykes, Ducati were there with their regular factory effort and Nori Haga, Aprilia were finding their feet in the championship with Max Biaggi, and BMW were in the second year of their massive-budget effort with double champion Troy Corser. In my opinion, 2009 was the first year World Superbikes started to regain its former status as a world championship, with most of the major manufacturers involved, and I think my results gave Honda some hope we could fight for the title with the Ten Kate team.

As we constantly tried to develop the bike's performance – fine-tuning the base setting that we began each race weekend with, refining the power delivery to improve corner exit – I was still learning, as a rider, in the way I did with AP in the previous season, and got a huge schooling that year from Carlos Checa. It was amazing for me to understand his riding style and, by overlaying his data with mine, we could see he was doing things like rolling off the throttle without upsetting the bike, whereas I was perhaps a little more forceful. That was never more evident than at a flowing track like Salt Lake City, where he'd done the double the previous year and where we could see how he was being so smooth with the throttle, not just on acceleration but off the gas, too. I tended to be a bit more aggressive, especially in closing the throttle and braking, which could upset the balance of the bike going into corners.

So, in studying Carlos's data I was able to smooth out my style. It's still something I refer to now when I'm riding too aggressively, and I end up going back to Checa-style. Ironically, you need a bit of both sometimes and his smoothness may have something to do with why Checa never really got the Honda to work and why, when he jumped on the Ducati in the following years, he dominated and won the championship.

Thinking back, I'd say all my years with Honda definitely made me a better rider. One of the best assets I developed is an ability to adapt my style subconsciously. That is not always best for the development of a motorcycle, but I can jump on a bike, for example, with soft or hard suspension and generally understand within a lap or two what rider inputs are needed. That ability to adapt can actually make it hard to find a clear direction for development, because my instinct is to make whatever I'm riding go faster by riding it, rather than by understanding the technical reasons why it's not going fast enough. Ronald pulled me to one side at Phillip Island one year after I'd ridden a few slow laps and said, 'Listen, this is a world championship. I don't pay all that money for fuel and tyres for you to ride slowly.' From that day I have put 100% into every lap I ride, and even if things aren't quite right, I try to put everything into it to at least make a lap time and make it as fast as I can to understand my rhythm.

When we were going through one of our rough patches, the team's technical manager Pieter Breddels said, 'Things aren't going to get better. This is what you have, so we're not going to touch the bike for this session. Go out and do a race simulation and you'll find the speed and understand the bike better.' That philosophy has stuck with me and I rate myself now as one of the hardest-working riders during practice.

I'm still constantly working on race simulations and understanding how the bike changes over 20 laps. For a start, the character and performance of the Pirelli tyre changes a lot between lap one and lap 21. The fuel load goes from 24 litres down to one or two, which changes the weight and balance of the bike, affecting how it handles. Those changing factors make it so difficult to set the bike up perfectly and precisely for a race. I always feel I can be more productive understanding how the bike performance changes during the race than I can sitting in the garage going through detailed technicalities to try to find a single fast lap in qualifying.

My years in motocross helped too, because the amount of rider inputs that can alter the performance of the bike is huge. It's nothing that you'd be able to see on TV or even from the side of the track, but there are a lot of little tricks that apply to riding a Superbike, especially around really challenging circuits like Portimao. They can be little changes to your body position and riding style as the tyre begins to go off during the race. You can't attack the track in those conditions like you would early on in a race, when the grip level is higher. On the other hand, it's maybe easier for other people, who haven't been riding motocross since the age of six, to be fast on smoother, more conventional circuits.

I guess people were noticing I was riding well, because in addition to that Yamaha offer in 2009, I was also approached by Bertie Hauser of BMW. They had arrived in World Superbikes the previous year as the new, big-budget team in the paddock and their hospitality unit probably cost more to run than the entire Honda team. They were desperate for me to ride their new S1000RR machine, but I had a buyout clause in my contract of something like £750,000. In financial terms it was huge and, from an ethical point of view, it was impossible, especially at my age and level of experience. But it didn't stop BMW throwing a two-year, £1.2-million deal on the table. They weren't prepared to buy me out of my Honda contract, but they were more than happy to give me that money so I could do it myself.

It was tempting. I was 22, still in my rookie season in World Superbikes. But, as we headed towards the 2010 season with a new team-mate in German Max Neukirchner, it did start to feel like I was steering the development of the bike and that I was building the team around me. Carlos was off to Ducati, Kiyonari was heading back to BSB and I wasn't ready to upset the momentum I felt we had built in the bike's development. I ended up fifth in the championship in 2009, in spite of the problems at the beginning of the season.

One thing I knew as we headed towards the end of 2009 was that I needed to get away from Northern Ireland and the feud that was starting to develop between my parents. I knew my team-mate Andrew Pitt lived in this cool little world on the Isle of Man, riding his bicycle and being a professional athlete, so I started planning with Chuck and International Racers to relocate there. I knew the place was quite popular with other motorsport people like James Toseland, Dougie Lampkin, Neil Hodgson and others, so I decided it was probably time for me to invest there too. But it would have been the same effect if I had moved to Switzerland, or Monaco, or even Andorra where a lot of other riders base themselves. I'm lucky that my business is conducted in 13 or 14 different countries around the world, so I could have set up my racing company anywhere. I chose the Isle of Man because my dad took me there loads of times when I was young and he was racing there. It's relatively close to Northern Ireland, too.

Neil Hodgson introduced me to a local guy called Gavin Hunt. His dad, Paul, had raced against my dad back in the day, and Gav was a really good British Superstock rider in his own right and raced in the 2013 TT. We hit it off straight away and Gav has since become a true and valuable friend to me and he's one of the first people I call after a race weekend. Like my coach, Fabien Foret, he's also one of the people around me who's not scared to tell me to wind my neck in or to let me know when he thinks I haven't been riding well.

Gav is a firefighter now, but he used to be a carpenter and joiner, so he's really handy. Above all we share a love of bikes and Gav always comes on my pre-season motocross camp in Spain.

I WAS SO excited by the 2010 season, we were building a challenge for the championship – but then it all kicked off at Assen.

Assen is a favourite of most riders because it's so fast, which usually produces very close races. It's a historic place where they've been racing motorcycles for something like 80 years and the local fans are very knowledgeable. They mostly try to watch at the final chicane – the Gert Timmer – which is a good overtaking place and has a tendency to produce a lot of drama at the end of a race. It's also rammed on race days, so it's a very special place to stop and interact with the crowd after winning a race, which I've been lucky enough to do on a few occasions.

It's an incredible place to win for a Dutch team. All the support staff at the team's workshop and the dealership, who don't normally get to the races, come and enjoy themselves with their families. The team also builds a balcony at the back of the garage, so anyone in the paddock can come in during sessions and look directly down on the team at work. I scored my first double there in 2010, which was just the most magical experience.

The rest of the season went pretty smoothly. I had gone into it fit and healthy and the bike was strong, too. I was making fewer mistakes and beginning to find some consistency. I took a win and a second place at Brno and went 2–2 at Nürburgring, with other podiums at Portimao, Kyalami and Donington Park.

We went into the last two rounds in third and not much more than a stone's throw away from Max Biaggi, who was leading the championship. The penultimate race was at one of the most iconic venues in world motorsport, Imola, which sits in a beautiful park near the centre of this historic Italian city. The weather there is usually perfect, but Superpole was wet, and Imola is notorious for its low grip levels in those conditions. On my first flying lap, approaching the first of Imola's four chicanes, I flicked the bike from left to right and had a massive highside. This was probably influenced by the fact that the circuit doesn't have many right-hand turns meaning, in the wet especially, it's hard to generate heat on the right side of the tyre to provide the grip you need. As soon as I touched the throttle, the rear let go and then gripped again. I was launched into the air, landing on my left shoulder and slapping the back of my wrist into the tarmac. I knew something was wrong straight away. Sure enough, I had separated my left shoulder and torn the ligament between the scaphoid and lunate bones in my left wrist.

The Clinica Mobile – a mobile clinic in the paddock that follows the World Superbike Championship – did a good job trying to get me out the following day and, with a pain-killing injection and a lot of physiotherapist's tape, we wanted to try to race. I crashed again in warm-up, fortunately without aggravating anything, but I couldn't ride properly so we decided it would be safer to withdraw me. I was distraught and felt all the hard work we had done had been for nothing.

I did the only thing I knew and switched the focus of my racer's brain to recovery and a return to racing as quickly as possible. Darren Roberts got me to Manchester to see a hand specialist, Mike Hayton, to see if I could finish the season. My wrist needed an operation, but he agreed to make me a hard plastic cast to race in the final round of the championship at Magny-Cours two weeks later. While Leon Haslam was still battling Biaggi for the title, Carlos Checa was right behind me in the championship, fighting for third. A top three finish in my second championship would be a great result and Honda still paid a decent third-place bonus. I went out in race one at Magny-Cours but, even with the extra support from the cast, the incredible forces that go through the arms and wrists under braking and acceleration meant I just couldn't ride properly. Through tears and gritted teeth, I got four points for 12th in the first race but the pain was too much to take part in race two. Carlos took third place from me by five points but, to their credit, Honda paid me the third-place bonus anyway.

Looking back on that season now, I'm sure if I was the rider I am today we could have really challenged for the title. And in spite of the injury, the year ended with some optimism – with four wins it was still my best season yet.

There are always key moments you look back on and think maybe you could have played that differently or that you shouldn't have made that mistake. But then again, if every corner of every lap was perfect, racing would soon get pretty boring. A few more victories would have made a big difference to my championship challenge in 2010, and I think the bike was definitely capable of that. But the season ended in a lot of pain, too. When I broke my femur in 2004, racing wasn't my job. Imola was the first time I'd suffered a bad injury as a full-time professional. Now I had a winter to recover and rehabilitate in the Isle of Man, so it was time to get to work.

CHAPTER 10

HONDA GRIND

TATIA WESTON HAS played a huge part in my life for the past 10 years and more. She was brought up in Cowes on Phillip Island, Australia – the town nearest to the famous racing circuit – and she got into bike racing when World Superbikes were there one year, back in the day. She was about 18 and doing a holiday job as a waitress in a local Italian restaurant when Neil Tuxworth, then the Castrol Honda team manager, asked her to come and work for him. She wanted to see the world and reckoned this was a pretty good opportunity to get paid while doing just that.

I think what first drew me to Tatia was her maturity and her honesty. Although we came from opposite ends of the world, she understood everything about the racing world that I grew up in, she understood how boys were and there'd be no story you could tell Tatia that would shock her. She'd had this whirlwind existence before I met her, and she'd travelled the world, gathering a load of life experience, which was exactly what I needed when I made the jump to world championship level in 2008. I think I can sum up my feelings most accurately by saying that before I found my girlfriend, and then my wife, I found a best friend.

It was while she was my friend – way before the point where I couldn't imagine spending my life with anyone else – that I learned about all her qualities. She knew my entire story before we became 'official', it was pretty much an open book. We talked about our previous relationships and actually counted them up – thankfully the numbers were quite similar, so there were no skeletons in the cupboard. I was pretty happy for our relationship to find its legs, but when Tatia came back from Australia at the beginning of 2010 planning to work for Paul Bird again, I said to her, 'Look, you can do your job from anywhere in the world. Why don't you come over to Northern Ireland and do it from here, living with me?' I cleared half my wardrobe and she moved in, and a few months later we both moved into the apartment in Castletown on the Isle of Man.

I had the girl of my dreams and 2010 turned into one of the best seasons with Honda, but I knew it wasn't easy for Tatia. She had gone through a bit of a culture shock, leaving a beautiful, sunny island in Australia to come to a wet and windy island in the middle of the Irish Sea. While I had been sold on the Isle of Man dream for a while and had met some really nice people there, like Gavin Hunt, Tatia hated it from day one and it took her a long time to feel any sense of belonging. At the same time, Birdy had switched manufacturer and the fact I was riding for Honda and my girlfriend was working for a Kawasaki team created some tensions, so she stopped at the end of that season.

Obviously, she had amazing memories of her life before she left Australia, a life of sunshine and sandy beaches. It was made pretty clear to me that while my life was great, she thought I'd properly messed up hers! But I felt that I'd kind of rescued her from a pretty shit existence with Birdy's team.

After my wrist injury at the end of 2010, I was lucky enough to find an incredible physio on the Isle of Man called Isla Scott. She's a freak with injuries and it was like she really relished the challenge of the major rehab I needed. I went into the hyperbaric chamber daily – sometimes twice a day – and I saw Isla every other day. When you are sidelined, you're out of sight, out of mind, meaning the comeback needs to be strong. The fact the injury was on my left wrist was a bit of a saviour, because it's much less important than an injury to the other side, which you use for throttle and brake. So I had two external pins holding the two bones together – the lunate and the scaphoid – and the ligament was grafted between the two. After some time in a pot, or cast, to stabilise it, I was straight into the physiotherapy to get ready for the new season.

Part of that rehab programme turned out to be an invitation to test Honda's RCV212V MotoGP machine at Sepang in Malaysia. Casey Stoner had just signed from Ducati and I was being asked to provide my input into the development of the 2011 bike, still quite an honour despite my reservations about HRC. It was also an opportunity to learn a new circuit and ride a GP machine in a no-pressure environment. I rode alongside Kousuke Akiyoshi, HRC's official test rider who I had teamed up with the year before for another Suzuka 8 Hours effort which saw us get on the box in third.

There was a load of new parts to test plus HRC's new secret weapon, the seamless gearbox. The whole experience was really taking the technical side of things to another level. Superbikes are derived from showroom sports bikes, heavily modified for racing, but a MotoGP bike is a pure thorough-bred, developed for one thing and one thing only: to race. It's the two-wheeled equivalent of a Formula 1 car. I loved the bike and took to it pretty fast, and I especially loved being faster than Akiyoshi.

It was also my first chance to work with a different crew since I joined Ten Kate in 2008. It was pretty much the crew that helped Casey Stoner win the MotoGP Championship the following year, and it was fascinating to hear different viewpoints on bike set-up and learn about technology that was new to me.

The problem was I could barely string ten laps together. I was having to stop riding to ice my wrist for half an hour and get the swelling down. Honda were cool about it because I'd told them about the problem, and they even flew my mate Keith Amor out to look after me.

After the good results in 2010, I wanted to come back super-strong for 2011 and there was a renewed buzz and energy in the team. I had a new team-mate in Ruben Xaus and Castrol became our title sponsor, which brought back memories of the earlier Castrol Honda team that won three World Superbike titles with John Kocinski back in 1996 and with Colin Edwards in 2000 and 2002 – including that epic last-round battle at Imola with Troy Bayliss, which is still probably the best race I've ever seen.

I'd ridden the Suzuka 8 Hours bike a lot the previous year, during testing and in the race, and one of the biggest differences between that bike and ours in World Superbikes was that it was so smooth and easy to ride, because of the electronics. I'd been trying to look for a similar feeling but, while most Superbike teams were using Magneti Marelli electronics on their bikes, we were the only team using the PI system. So it became my focus for the 2011 season to get the electronics right, and I felt if we could get hold of the HRC software from the Suzuka 8 bike then we could make some progress and do a good job.

They sent a couple of Japanese engineers early on, but it quickly became apparent they seriously undervalued what we were up to with Honda in World Superbikes and thought they had better ideas on what we should be doing. Also, the parameters of the PI system we used were actually far superior to what we could change on the kit electronics HRC had sent, so we quickly outgrew it. The support from Japan was terrible and, with hindsight, I wish we'd never gone down that route because we spent the first part of that 2011 season completely lost, in spite of another win and a third at Assen.

As I pushed to get what I could out of the bike, I crashed in successive races at Monza and at Miller in the USA, but even when I was finishing a race, the results weren't what we were there for. We got to Misano in Italy still searching for an electronics breakthrough and I was just not enjoying riding. We weren't moving forward with the bike at all and it felt like we were stuck in rut. I didn't even want to be there.

My wish got answered the very next day.

Turn 11 at Misano is the super-fast Curvone, a fifth gear, flat-out, 160mph right-hander, and during a qualifying lap I went out a little too wide on the exit and hit the green AstroTurf which was still damp from overnight dew. It was one of the biggest crashes of my career and, as I finally came to a rest after being fired through the gravel trap, I knew straight away I had a problem with my wrist – this time my right one. It was the same injury I'd had the year before and required the same reconstructive surgery, although it was slightly more complicated because I broke my radius bone as well. I knew my season was effectively over. I also knew exactly what the rehab would involve and how long it was going to take, so I went back to the Isle of Man to sit on the couch and get back to work with Isla.

In the first half of 2011, things were still tough for Tatia but it turned around after I got injured again at Misano. I think the period of my rehab made us tighter, because Tatia was the only one helping me. She drove me to the hyperbaric chamber every morning and to all my physio sessions. My parents were still going through the divorce process at home, so they had their own issues; I'd been having a really hard time with the bike and the team in Superbike, so the two of us were thrown together more closely than ever and I realised I wanted to spend the rest of my life with her. So, when I was passing through Gatwick airport on one trip, I met a good friend of mine, Philip Coulter, who was a jeweller. He brought down a selection of rings from London and I bought one from him there and then.

I hid the ring for ages next to the battery under the seat in the van I used for motocross. I was paranoid the whole time that if the van got stolen or caught fire I could lose this quite expensive diamond ring. So eventually I took her to this lovely hotel in the middle of a forest – she's really into nature and loves trees – where I'd planned this romantic proposal during a walk. It was the night before I was due to have another operation on my wrist and it started chucking it down with rain, so we couldn't get out of the hotel. I was really starting to panic about making this proposal, I was so nervous; plus I was going under the knife the next day. Tatia had kind of taken over my life with booking flights and hotels and I was terrified that she might find the ring, which was now stuffed in my backpack, while I was having my operation.

So I built up the courage to propose and, although it wasn't quite the romantic forest setting that I'd planned, we got quite emotional and I think we both shed a tear as she said yes. The worst part, though, was that the ring was completely the wrong size. She had this kind of wooden hand ornament that she kept all her rings on at home and I thought I was being quite clever by taking a ring she didn't wear very much and getting it sized. I got the engagement ring made but I'd stolen the wrong ring – it was one that she wore on her middle finger! Tatia kept telling me that the ring was so beautiful, but it was massive and as we sat through dinner that night she had to keep squeezing her fingers together to stop it falling off. We ended up hiding it in a matchbox and posting it back to Philip to get it made smaller, even though no-one would insure it. But it all worked out and that was us engaged. I think it was the step our relationship needed and Tatia started to feel a lot more secure and we became more supportive of each other. She was still struggling a bit with the Isle of Man, but we felt like more of a team and more comfortable talking about our future and about starting a family.

That injury turned out to be a blessing in a lot of ways. I had not been enjoying riding the bike and at home I watched the races on TV. My team-mate, Xaus, and replacement rider, Alex Lowes, didn't do anything on the bike and it looked like it was trying to throw them off in the same way it had been trying to launch me.

One technical disadvantage was our bike was still using a cable throttle. Most of our competitors were using fly-by-wire technology by that stage – a system that sends a precise digital signal from the throttle to the engine, rather than a mechanical one – which gave them much more accurate control over fuelling and power delivery. The rules said you had to use what was homologated on the production model and the Honda CBR was still sold with a cable throttle, so our set-up was a bit like what you'll find on a lawnmower: you twist the throttle which pulls a cable and you go. But while I was away with the injury, the organisers changed the rules so we were allowed to add fly-by-wire for better electronic control.

After missing eight races, I got back on the bike in Germany and had a tough weekend with a tenth and a fourth, but after that we tested the new throttle system at

Assen. The test was productive, nothing spectacular, but there must be something with me and new developments because we rocked up at Imola and won straight away.

We were able to make the acceleration much more precise and, where we needed to take power away to stop losing grip, we could do it much more smoothly. There was also a massive difference when I was stopping the bike. I no longer needed to use the clutch to backshift gears; as soon as I put pressure on the gear lever with my left foot the new system automatically blipped the throttle and cut the power as I went down through the gears. Everything was so much smoother and it was not only less physically challenging during the race, it was less stressful on your brain. Suddenly, I could just concentrate on my braking marker and finding the apex. I took a lot of pride in single-handedly developing the system.

At Imola we pretty much dominated race one, riding away from Nori Haga, and I was all set to double up in race two when a sensor worth about 50p broke and the bike stopped, taking me out of the lead and the race. The same problem happened the following week in race two at Magny-Cours, where I had qualified on pole and made my own mistake in the first race, crashing out of the lead early on with a ridiculous gap of about ten seconds. But we went to Portimao for the last round and got a double podium there, plus a couple of wins from earlier in the season went some way to salvaging what had been a really difficult year for a number of reasons.

* * *

AS WE WENT into 2012, I'd lost a bit of faith in my crew chief, so the team's technical manager Pieter Breddels moved into the chair next to mine in the garage. Pieter was a suspension specialist but was also being groomed to take over from Ronald as team manager, so this was seen as a way to give him wider team experience. After continuing to work hard through the winter on rehab for my wrist, we entered the new season with fresh motivation. I picked up a couple of wins, one in Assen, which was becoming a happy hunting ground, and another at Donington Park. There were some other podium finishes, but the overall results were not enough for me to finish any higher than fifth in the championship, like in 2009.

It was a year to forget, apart from the Suzuka 8 Hours. Honda always looked after me when I went to ride there – they gave us business class flights and a nice hotel at the circuit and it was the perfect distraction for me to go and actually feel loved, which I wasn't getting as a Ten Kate Superbike rider. There was never any need to take a personal assistant, because they'd always have someone literally to take the helmet off your head and take it to the Arai technicians. The race always takes place just after the rainy season, so the temperature is usually in the mid-30s with humidity around 85%, so there were also people to dry your leathers out. There were physiotherapists to give you a massage between sessions, nutritionists, the lot – full factory pampering, basically, and I really enjoyed that.

I'd already had some experience of the race and it is, without question, the single toughest challenge I've ever done in my life. It's also an incredibly important event to Honda.

The racing is brutal – absolutely brutal – not helped by the fact Honda only run with two riders in their official team while most other teams use three. I was so excited to sign up to do it again, but after the first hour on the bike you're thinking, 'What the hell am I doing here?' You get an hour from stepping off the bike to getting back on it, and in that time you have to get out of your leathers and go straight into the ice bath to lower your core temperature. Then you try to take some food and fluids on board to rehydrate, usually eating while you're on the massage table getting any niggles ironed out. You're called back to the garage to be ready for a changeover 15 minutes before the pit-stop.

Then there's the sheer heat that comes off the bike which starts to burn your body, especially your feet, and Alpinestars had to insulate my boots really heavily. My right boot was just over the exhaust, so they fixed some gold-plated material to the sole to deflect some of the heat.

It's a real team effort, too. In Superbike, when the lights go out after working with my team all weekend, it's basically down to me to go and get the result. In the Suzuka 8, there are so many people involved right the way through, including the crew who change wheels and refuel at every pit-stop. And when I say pit-stop, they could change front and rear wheels in six seconds, then, five seconds later, you were full of fuel and heading down the pit-lane again.

The emotion involved is incredible. It's not called 'endurance' for nothing. The bike is being pushed to its maximum performance and engine stress for eight hours solid – in some other races in the championship, it's 24 hours. Riding like that in 36°C, with a 50–60°C track temperature and very high humidity is pretty stressful on the rider, too, and you can lose around 1.5kg in body weight during an hour on the bike. It's like riding your bicycle in a sauna for an hour. The weight loss is pretty much all down to fluids. Riders used to go on IV drips to get the fluids back in, but they're banned now.

It's the only race where you see grown men cry. When my team-mate Kousuke Akiyoshi crashed out of the race in 2013, Honda's senior project leader burst into tears in front of everyone in the team because he'd invested so much time and passion into the programme.

I'm always nervous before a race, even to this day, but I'm never as nervous as I am before the Suzuka 8 Hours because so many things can go wrong. You have a team-mate, so you're also worried about letting them and everyone else down. My team-mate in 2012 was Akiyoshi again and although his English wasn't great it was good enough to reassure me everything was fine and I should just enjoy myself. I sort of fed off how cool he was and, although I was cramping really badly in my legs in my final stint, after eight hours of hard racing Akiyoshi rode the last hour and brought it home. We got the job done and I also had the incredible feeling of pride being the first British rider to win the race. I remember being so happy that Tatia was also there to enjoy what was an unbelievable experience. I knew how impor-tant the event was to Honda, and that win in 2012 remains the best victory of my career, but it's also a huge money earner. And it's kind of whetted my appetite for endurance racing after I've finished in World Superbikes. I'd love to do a 24-hour race.

After that amazing Suzuka experience, we were at a Superbike race in Russia towards the end of August. I'd had a tip-off from Chris Hillard, who worked for Alpinestars but later went on to become Casey Stoney's PA, that Stoner had broken his ankle in a MotoGP qualifying crash in America and was going to miss at least two rounds. If a rider is out for more than one race, the team has to find a replacement and my name was being put out there as a candidate. It was flattering, of course, but I had this Moscow event to focus on. However, during the weekend, the guys from Honda sat me down in the office and asked me if I'd be interested.

We weren't strong in 2012 and we certainly weren't battling for the championship, so it was an amazing opportunity. MotoGP was racing at Brno the same weekend we were in Russia and the guys told me there was a test the day after the Brno MotoGP race, which would give me a chance to ride the bike and find my feet, then I'd be racing at Misano and possibly Aragon two weeks later. The problem was it was going to be back-to-back with Superbike races – five consecutive weekends swapping from Honda's CBR1000 in Superbike on Pirelli tyres to Honda's RCV213V in MotoGP on Bridgestones. It was pretty tough to get my head round, but I just thought, 'Well, I've got nothing to lose, so why not?' They were going to pay me a bit of extra money; the

MotoGP bonuses were great, even for a top ten finish. The issue was getting from Moscow on the Sunday night to Brno in the Czech Republic for the test the following morning, so we drove pretty much all night between airports to get there.

I was just Stoner's replacement – essentially going out to fulfil sponsor and team contracts – so there shouldn't really have been any pressure on me. But when I got to the track late the following morning, after everyone else had started testing at 9.00, the first person I saw in the paddock was Shuhei Nakamoto, the vice-president of HRC who I'd met at the Suzuka 8 Hours a month before. The first thing he said, in his jokey little laughing voice, was 'Have fun, but don't crash!'

If that made me feel bad, it only got worse when I first stared down the barrel that was the back of the bike in the garage. It was dripping in carbon fibre, like a technical piece of art. I had always joked with myself that, if I ever made a mistake and crashed my Ten Kate bike into a brick wall, I'd say, 'My fault – I'll pay for the damage.' But this RCV213V looked like it was worth more money than me and everything I'd ever owned. So I had a strange fear of the bike, a fear of crashing it, and I wish Nakamoto hadn't planted the seed because that fear never really left me the whole time I rode the RCV.

I was so stiff I didn't feel I was able to display my full potential. I'd ridden Honda's MotoGP machine at the end of 2010, but I remember leaving the pit-lane in Brno thinking, 'This bike is so SLOW …!' Honestly, when I opened the gas, it was like a pussycat – it felt like I could lean it over to

60 degrees, crank the throttle open and nothing would happen until the bike decided to let me have it. The animal that I was expecting was actually quite easy to ride, but very difficult to ride fast. While I could understand the bike and what it was doing, I really didn't understand the limits of the Bridgestone tyres, especially the front. I had some experience of using Bridgestones at the Suzuka 8, but the MotoGP tyre was completely different, and of course a world away from the Pirellis I was using in World Superbikes. To get the MotoGP bike to turn, I had to use a load more rear brake than I was used to, while keeping pressure on the front tyre to keep it deformed all the way to the apex so it would turn in. It was completely illogical to me and went against everything my dad had told me all those years ago at my Red Bull Rookie test at Rockingham, which was basically to get all the braking done before you turn in. Now, when I was releasing the brake, the tyre was reforming, completely changing the contact patch and stopping the bike from turning. My data guy and the crew were trying to encourage me to use two bar of extra braking pressure and crank the bike over an extra couple of degrees, but my brain kept telling me I was going to crash. And that's exactly what Nakamoto had told me not to do.

The bike's fuelling and the way it delivered its power was not that much different to my Superbike – in fact the CBR accelerated much faster than the RCV and that's something we still see today in the end-of-year test at Jerez in Spain, when MotoGP machines share the track with World Superbikes. While initial acceleration is quite similar, the

real difference with a MotoGP bike is how the speed continues to build as they really find their legs in fourth, fifth and
sixth gears and the rpm level just keeps on climbing. But it
wasn't only how quick they went, it was how quick they
stopped with carbon brakes and the Bridgestone front tyre,
and that was the toughest thing to manage in my brain, and
I didn't have a lot of time to learn.

It was not helped by the fact both my MotoGP races at
Misano and Aragon were wet or damp throughout free
practice. It was the end of the summer season in Misano
when it should have been baking hot, and the first time I
really rode the bike in anger was in qualifying, which was a
huge eye opener as I hadn't yet found its limits.

I'd never really got comfortable enough to push the bike
hard and it was difficult to suddenly go out and put it all on
the line in qualifying. But as soon as I started to wind it up a
bit for the first time in the dry, I knew I hadn't even got close
to what this bike was capable of. I honestly don't think I got
close to its limit during the whole MotoGP experience.

I qualified on the third row alongside Ben Spies on the
factory Yamaha, which I felt was OK, but my biggest fear,
even though I was a complete rookie, was getting beaten by
a CRT bike, a class within MotoGP for independent teams.
I was super-nervous lining up for the race against guys like
Dani Pedrosa, Valentino Rossi and Jorge Lorenzo, but I'd
beaten other riders like Cal Crutchlow in 2010. He had
made the switch to MotoGP a couple of years earlier and
had some success, albeit really slowly in his second and third
years. I was still on a steep learning curve though, so I didn't

know what to expect in the way of results. I had a pretty lonely race chasing down Nicky Hayden on the factory Ducati – the gap stayed constant. Another thing I learned quickly was that the character of the Bridgestones didn't change during the race. If a gap appeared after two or three laps, it was difficult to chase these guys down because they didn't make mistakes and you couldn't make it up when the grip levels dropped because the drop was consistent. But I finished eighth. I was pretty happy and expecting a little more going into Aragon.

There was a bit of talk back then that the Gresini MotoGP team might be interested in me. It came mostly from the commercial director of the Repsol Honda team, Livio Suppo, who I put a lot of faith and trust in. He was telling me that Fausto Gresini was looking for a rider to replace Alvaro Bautista. However, the main team sponsor, an energy drink, had been at that Misano race and Bautista had stuck the bike on the podium and both he and the sponsor re-signed for the team that night in all the excitement and enthusiasm.

At Aragon I qualified seventh, again in wet and patchy conditions throughout practice, apart from one dry session when I did a pretty good job. My data guy came to me that night and said he'd been speaking with Valentino Rossi's crew who had said he was predicting he'd be racing against me based on our relative race pace. It made me feel full of confidence that Rossi was considering me as his pace marker that weekend, even though that was during his unsuccessful year with Ducati. I couldn't believe how aggressive everyone was at the start of the race and I set off with Bautista, who duffed me up a bit at turn seven and I couldn't make up the gap for the rest of the race. I finished one place behind him in seventh.

Don't get me wrong, the whole experience was incredible – the racing was fun, and I enjoyed working with the crew and learned a lot from Christian Gabbarini, Stoner's very methodical, quietly spoken Italian engineer.

Gabbarini has worked with some really good riders and I was intrigued to know whether he made a difference to their riding. These bikes are so powerful, the front wheel can lift off the ground in virtually any gear at any speed. Christian taught me to prevent wheelies by pulling my weight forward at the right times rather than relying on the electronic wheelie control, which kills the power for micro seconds and can reduce drive and acceleration out of a corner.

The entire team seemed to be geared around the rider. I had my own private office in one of the technical trucks and anything I asked for, like an extra hotel room or a couple more passes, they would sort without question. I'm not a cheapskate, but I remember at Misano they'd booked me a really high-level hire car. I normally go for one level above compact, just in case I have a crash, then at least I'll stand a better chance of surviving. Simple things like the level of hospitality in the MotoGP paddock were also an unbelievable pleasure – the cuisine was amazing, the amount of different options for dinner blew my mind. Even Alpinestars had their own hospitality in the paddock and it was back when the BBC was still covering MotoGP, so everything felt like a really big deal with a strong British influence and I felt very much at home there. The two race weekends were very special and definitely whetted my appetite to go back. I felt I was able to demonstrate my talent and, when I draw comparisons, not many rookies have jumped into MotoGP with two top ten finishes. Yes, I was on a proven bike, but I'd hardly ridden it and I was competing with riders who had years of experience and who were in the second half of their season, with countless races and tests behind them.

So, although 2012 was another disappointing year with Superbike results and the development of the Honda CBR, at least I stayed injury free. And there were some incredible racing highlights and awesome experiences, like winning the Suzuka 8 Hours and joining the Repsol Honda MotoGP team, for a short while at least.

CHAPTER 11

LITTLE FEET, ITCHY FEET

TATIA AND I soon set a wedding date in the middle of a busy racing season, and we got married in the Lake District on 7 July 2012. Australia was too far for important guests like Nanna and the McCammonds, so the Lakes, as well being totally beautiful, was also a kind of neutral territory. In typical fashion we fell out a couple of nights before because, after months of planning, Tatia suddenly wanted to change the layout and the order of the speeches, while I had quite a straightforward, traditional event in my head.

It turned out to be a perfect day, though. When Tatia told me a couple of days before that Mum, Dad, Richard, Kristofer and Chloe were going to go to the church together, I started crying because I had my perfect little family back. It was so great to have them together for the day, even though my parents were still going through their messy divorce.

As I write this nearly ten years after the split, I'd say things with my parents are just about back to a situation where everyone is OK with how things are. I know that my ideal family is not going to come back, but things are much more relaxed now for everyone. We've even been out to dinner with Mum, Dad and his partner Sandra, who's a lovely lady and does amazingly to put up with him and to keep his life ticking along. Now the whole family is on a WhatsApp group together and there's even a joke on there between my parents every now and again, which nobody really bites on because they can be below the belt! But it's as good as it's been for a long time.

Tatia enjoyed a few drinks that night – I remember her shouting at my Nanna across the room about what a night she was going to give me! A couple of weeks later we moved into our matrimonial home, a lovely new townhouse 200 metres down the road from our old apartment in Castletown on the Isle of Man.

Tatia and I share similarly strong family values and, like me, she was born into a loving and close family. We have all shared lots of amazing times together on the other side of the world. Tatia's been a massive support to me in my racing, because she's very real and keeps my feet firmly on the ground. She's not the sport's biggest fan so she doesn't get too caught up in the emotion of it. Sometimes I wish she was a little more into it, and there are times before a race when I'd love her to be out there on the grid with me, whispering encouragement in my ears, rather than being the shy quiet one, thinking the worst in the back of the garage. There are moments, too, when I'd really like to imagine her on the back of the bike with me, pushing me to make a pass.

As we went into 2013, we had something else incredibly exciting to think about: Tatia was pregnant and I was going to become a dad. I was super-excited at the prospect and at the idea of building a little family unit like the one I had enjoyed so much as a child. The problem was her due date coincided with the Laguna Seca World Superbike round in the USA and, while it was kind of frowned upon, we even started to make some enquiries about getting her induced early, so I could be at the birth and make the race.

ON THE TRACK, it felt like we were coming to the end of the line in the development of the Honda CBR. To stay at Honda for 2013, I had asked them to hire my old BSB crew chief, Chris Pike. There was one problem: Chris wasn't Dutch. Their mechanics mainly came from their own dealership in Nieuwleusen and, for more technical roles like electronics, from Dutch universities. Chris's arrival meant tearing up their rule book and I had to fight really hard to get him onboard. But I had huge respect for him from our time in BSB where we had a lot of fun together.

It was a huge decision for him to leave a cosy job in the UK and rejoin the World Superbike circus. He'd been there and done it more than ten years before as a data guy for Colin Edwards when he was winning his world championships, so his credentials were pretty impressive. When we made it happen, I was delighted.

With Chris on board, I had eyes and ears on the team and was getting an honest opinion on what was possible. If I was kicking and screaming about something not being right, Chris could tell me straight: he could come to me and say it couldn't be changed, or he could say, 'Let me manage this and fix it.'

At Ten Kate, the whole idea of building a relationship between the rider and his crew chief was actively discouraged. Talking to people in the team since I left has confirmed this as true: riders come and go so you shouldn't get friendly with them outside the circuit. But having Chris in there was really the first step towards building what would eventually become Team65.

Decent results were hard to come by in the first part of 2013, but I had podium finishes at Assen, Portimao and Imola. At Silverstone in early August, I won race one and got fourth in race two, and it felt like things could be turning round for the back end of the championship.

I was having discussions with other teams to see what options might be available, and midway through the season I had spoken with Kawasaki for the first time. They were leading the championship with Tom Sykes, who had missed the title by just half a point the year before. After sharing a track with him for many years, I had seen the level of Tom's riding and how good the Kawasaki ZX-10R was.

They had also promoted a rookie, Loris Baz, from Superstock and even he had won a race at Silverstone that year, which confirmed the bike was a weapon. From what I was hearing, though, Loris was a little hard to manage and it seemed a place in the team could be materialising. I spent some time chatting with the team manager, Guim Roda, but the offer they put on the table was a little bit disrespectful so I turned that down.

After Silverstone we went to Nürburgring in Germany feeling more confident. Following torrential rain in qualifying, the track dried on race day but the air was still heavy and it was very overcast. I started race one from fourth on the grid and I was still in fourth with around six laps to go – comfortable in the middle of a leading group of five or six riders, and in touch with Tom Sykes, who was leading. Suddenly, I saw red and yellow flags being waved, indicating the track might be slippery in that sector, probably because of oil. In a close group at those speeds, it's very difficult to see where the oil is on the tarmac, but as we headed up the hill towards the Schumacher S-curve I saw green flags waving, which meant the oil problem was clear.

I touched the brake for the fourth gear left-hander and suddenly I was down and sliding very fast towards the barriers. I've since seen a picture of myself heading into the tyre wall: my femur is straight but, unfortunately, it wasn't straight after I hit it. It was the same left femur I broke at Knockhill in 2004 and, again, the marshals pretty much diagnosed the injury as I was lying there.

As I lay in the circuit medical centre waiting for a helicopter to Koblenz Hospital, I just sank into a massive black mood. Tatia was at home and heavily pregnant. I was fed up with Honda and the lack of development of the bike and my season was finished. Kawasaki seemed to be a no-go for 2014 and there were no MotoGP teams knocking on my door. I was in tears.

Keith Amor put his life on hold for a few days for me. While his wife went to the Isle of Man to be with Tatia, he came with me to the hospital and did an amazing job keeping my spirits up.

I went straight into the operating theatre that night and had the same operation I'd had eight years previously – luckily the old pin had been taken out a few years before, because removing a bent pin would have been very complicated. After two days in a bed, I managed to haul myself into a chair to have a shower, but that completely drained me of all my energy.

Then the doctor came in, and God bless German doctors.

He said, 'Get up and on your feet.'

I reminded him, quite forcefully, I had just broken my femur.

'Get up,' he said. 'I am going to help you get out of bed.'

He pulled me up and, as I sat on the edge of the bed, he said, 'Stand up.'

I looked at him like he had four heads and thought to myself, 'How the hell does he expect me to stand up?'

He said, 'I've done a really good job with the pin and you'll be standing on that, not the bone. You can do it. We need you to start walking on it quickly, so we can generate activity in the area and speed up the healing process.'

This was getting stupid. The guy was expecting me to walk on a femur I broke badly just 48 hours before.

But he grabbed both my hands and helped me off the side of the bed. I put some weight through my left leg but was standing mostly on my right.

'I am going to let go of you. Walk towards me,' he said.

I took a few steps and there and then realised I was going to beat this injury.

A couple of days later, I hobbled out of the hospital on crutches and went straight home to the Isle of Man.

With all the trauma following the crash, it didn't occur to me that this might actually be a bit of a blessing. It was such a hard time for Tatia because she was heavily pregnant and needed a lot of support, too. But I wasn't able to give that too easily with my injury and because I was still up and down emotionally.

I missed the following round in Istanbul. Then, about four weeks after the crash, when I was supposed to be in Laguna Seca for the next race, Jake was born.

Tatia's labour was quite traumatic and although she elected to have a natural birth they ended up inducing her, which produced hours and hours of contractions that weren't doing anything. I ended up spending half the night on the floor next to her bed before, finally, the doctors rushed her off for an emergency caesarean.

After all the drama, though, and with Tatia exhausted, Jake came out as this perfect and amazingly strong and healthy 8lb 6oz little person.

Not only was I able to be there for his birth, but because of that German doctor's persistence I was able to fulfil one of my major ambitions and carry my son out of the hospital. And I got to take extended paternity leave to be with him and Tatia. Happy days.

There was no way I could have prepared myself for the effect that fatherhood was going to have on me – no father can. But being around those first few weeks was so special, and I immediately felt this impeccable bond with my new son.

If you'd asked me five years earlier if I wanted babies with me at race weekends, I'd have said absolutely not, no hesitation. But when this little fella came along and I spent those first months with him, no way was I leaving Jakey boy and Tatia behind for my next race. And having him around has made me even more determined to be successful – I want both my boys to be proud of me. Jake is still one of my biggest fans, the one who loves to be at my side at races and watch me win. Seeing his little face light up when I get back to parc fermé or when I'm stood on the podium, is the most precious thing and I'll keep it with me for ever.

OVER THOSE MONTHS I had some detailed discussions with Ducati. They'd matched the financial offer Honda was making and agreed I could take Chris Pike with me as my crew chief. There was a contract on the table waiting for my signature; our discussions had even got down to details like the new Audi Chris was getting as a company car.

At the same time Robert Watherston, motorsport manager of Honda Europe, was reminding me that we had passed a deadline he had given me to make a decision about staying with them. I told him if he needed a decision immediately, it would be no. He should talk to other riders if he wanted, I said, but don't back me into a corner after all the years I'd ridden with Honda.

Finally, Chuck and I agreed we were going to join Ducati. I just had to break the news to Ronald ten Kate, who I had already told that I'd been talking to other teams.

I was driving to yet another physio session in Douglas on the Isle of Man when I called Ronald on my hands-free.

I said, 'Ronald, it's been an amazing adventure coming to the world championships with you guys, but it's time for me to move on. I've reached an agreement with Ducati.'

In all my years with Ten Kate Honda, there was never any kind of heart-to-heart with Ronald, or him telling me how well he thought I was doing on the bike. We would have a beer after a win and celebrate, but he was never aware that I craved that kind of reassurance. Then suddenly, for the first time in six years, Ronald started talking to me like a human being. He was saying, 'Jonathan, you've done such an incredible job on the bike these last few years. Honestly, there's no way we would have had any of the success or wins we've had without your input.'

I told him I'd lost faith in the project, but he went on, 'Just look at the team-mates you've had, and they haven't got near you. Honda and this team need you and we've got a plan. We're so close and I honestly believe we can make that final step.' He started talking in detail about getting in a top data engineer, which I had been requesting all season.

Suddenly, I was beginning to feel valued for the first time. My head was still telling me to leave, but my heart was beginning to say 'stay'. I began to think that if I left, I would leave these people in the shit, and they were good guys. I started getting really emotional and I was crying as I said, 'Well … maybe we could give it one more season.' 'YES, YES!' Ronald screamed back down the phone. 'We'll put the things you need in place and let's give this one more go together!'

To this day I really don't know how he did it.

I called Chuck and asked him to burn the bridge I had painstakingly built over so many weeks with Ducati. They had gone above and beyond to try to get me to go there, and it's times like this when it really pays to have a manager to make those difficult calls. They ended up signing Chaz Davies for 2014.

My rehab for the broken femur had gone well and I'd made a good recovery, but I deliberately stayed away from all races including the final round of 2013, Jerez in Spain. Me and the team decided it would be better instead to take part in the end-of-season test on the following Monday.

The team had finally listened to me and brought on board a new electronics boffin – an Italian called Massimo Neri, who joined from the BMW team after the last race. He'd played an important role in the development of the BMW and, with Chris Pike, we suddenly had a deeper pool of knowledge to go into the following season. Looking back, this reinforced the start of what I've come to call Team65 – a collection of individuals who I work with that help to make everything tick. We started out on dual throttle-bodies during that winter test programme which allowed us to control the engine fuelling even more precisely.

We weren't expecting to be fast immediately and, when we got to Jerez, we were more than two seconds off Tom Sykes' lap times – a lifetime. He had just won the world championship, so he was the man of the moment.

At one point, I went out for a run on some fresh tyres and found myself behind him. In a practice or qualifying, you often find slower riders tagging on to the back of faster guys, following their lines and, if they're still close enough, slip-streaming down the straights.

I hadn't been planning on 'getting a tow' as it's called, but I thought it might be good to follow him for a couple of laps to compare his acceleration off the corner to ours, or his stability under braking. Tom hates being followed and towards the end of the first half of the lap he kept looking over his shoulder at me, then slowed right down to a snail's pace and waved me past. But by that point, I'd kind of committed myself to being a pest looking for a tow, so I stayed exactly where I was.

He went back into the pit-lane and I followed him and he kind of faked going back into the garage, but as he rode straight through I went back out and followed him for another lap. Tom was even more frustrated by this time, while I was just giggling in my helmet. After a few more corners, I thought he had probably had enough so I went past him and did a few laps before coming back to the garage for a debrief.

I had almost forgotten the whole incident and we were deep in a technical conversation when Tom stopped outside our garage and started gesticulating and shouting through his open visor. Chris went out to see what he was on about. I heard him shouting past Chris, 'Is he a professional or just a fucking amateur?'

To me, it was just hilarious that I'd wound up the world champion so much, considering we weren't a threat to him at all.

Winning the title changed Tom a bit. His acceptance speech was all about him having proved people wrong. He had this meteoric rise when Provec took over the official Kawasaki Superbike programme from Paul Bird in 2012. I think he had a bit of a chip on his shoulder, because no-one was ever really talking about him before then.

As we went into the new season, it was clear Massimo and Chris were working solidly together and I felt I was beginning to build a little bit of a team around me, as opposed to one that Ten Kate were imposing on me. I was incredibly motivated and fired up; everything and everyone came together pretty smoothly. I was super-consistent throughout the season and took four race wins, with another five podiums, and was only once outside a top six finish. We had no business racing for the championship that year, but I finished third and was only 82 points from Sylvain Guintoli's championship winning total.

Tom Sykes had a 44-point lead when we left Laguna Seca with three rounds and six races to go. At the next round in Jerez, he had one of his worst results of the season, and then we went to Magny-Cours where it was wet and he was riding like a rabbit caught in the headlights. His team-mate Loris Baz had to let him through at the last corner to finish fourth. Even that didn't stop the two of them falling out big time at the end of the season.

Maybe Tom had too much time to think about the championship after the summer break and chose the wrong strategy to ride defensively. He just started to ride tight and made it easy for Sylvain, as the hunter, to chase him down.

Sylvain had an incredible finish to the season and it all came down to the final race at the final round in Qatar. While Sylvain and I were relaxed and chilling by the hotel pool with our kids during the day, discussing how the night's races were going to pan out, I could just imagine Tom being holed up in his room with the pressure of the world on his shoulders.

I look back on my 2014 season at Honda knowing that in finishing third we punched well above our weight, and I ended up being really proud of what we achieved. I had Tatia and Jake at every race and that kind of re-lit my fire for racing again. I had less time to worry about stupid things you don't need to worry about, like other riders and what they were doing.

Sometimes in racing the more time you spend worrying about issues, the more problems you create, and 2014 turned into an enjoyable season – even though I knew it was the last effort I was going to make with Ten Kate Honda.

I'D BEEN HAVING more realistic discussions about moving to other World Superbike teams, but I was also still holding out some hope for the possibility of a MotoGP ride. I had kept in touch with Livio Suppo, the Repsol Honda commercial director, to sound out any possibilities as they arose.

When I first met Suppo, he had just found his way into Honda from Ducati's MotoGP team and followed Shuhei Nakamoto into the HRC hierarchy. Think of all the great double acts like Laurel and Hardy, Ant and Dec, Wallace and Gromit – well, Nakamoto and Suppo were nothing like any of them because Suppo just spent all his time blowing smoke up Nakamoto's arse. I'd been pretty disappointed with how little Nakamoto valued the efforts we were making in World Superbikes, but I figured out pretty quickly that to get to the top level in Honda, I had to win over the Nakamoto–Suppo double act.

In one of our chats, Suppo told me Lucio Cecchinello could be interested in me for his 2015 LCR Honda team.

Soon after, I was out cycling with Cal Crutchlow on the Isle of Man. He told me that despite having another year to run with Ducati, he was going to ride for Honda the following season. I figured out he was talking about that same LCR ride. So, I called Suppo and he told me to come to the Silverstone MotoGP race to talk to a few people.

At those meetings he said the LCR door was closed, then tried to talk me into riding one of the new Open Class bikes – saying it was 'such a great opportunity'. At that time in MotoGP, the CRT (Claiming Rule Team) or independent bikes were being phased out and Honda was building an 'Open Class' machine, which was supposed to make MotoGP more affordable for smaller, non-factory teams. The organisers were insisting there should be a price cap of a €1 million to buy the Open bike, whereas just leasing a full spec RCV from HRC was around €3 million.

I don't know how stupid these guys think we riders are, but Suppo pitched me that the €1 million Open Class bike could win races because of a dispensation to use softer tyres and carry more fuel. Yeah, right. Even with my limited commercial sense, I understood it would be pretty bad business to lease a bike for three million when one with the 'same performance' could be bought for one million. At the same time, he was telling me I couldn't expect to earn what I was getting in Superbike in MotoGP.

I said, 'Look, I want to come to MotoGP on a factory bike, but I'm happy to discuss taking a big cut in my salary to do it.' He looked at me as if I was a bit of dirt that he'd just scraped off his shoe and said, 'What makes you think you deserve a factory bike?' I just got up and walked out and that was the end of any talk about me going to MotoGP with Honda.

CHAPTER 12

END OF THE LINE

END OF THE LINE

AFTER OUR INITIAL Kawasaki meetings in 2013 and the offer I thought was a little below par, I had some more serious discussions with team manager Guim Roda during 2014. The year started as probably my best to date after I'd taken a win at Assen plus a double at Imola, so my Superbike CV was looking better than ever.

Kawasaki riders Tom Sykes and Loris Baz had been given options to renew, but Guim called me after a mid-season test and said both those deadlines had passed and Kawasaki were beginning to think outside the box. I said, 'OK, great, I'm coming to see you.'

I flew to Barcelona the next day, took a hire car and went to the team's workshop, but Guim immediately took me to a restaurant without even giving me a tour. Over lunch he introduced me to Pere Riba, who I'd raced against in the British Supersport Championship in 2004 and was potentially going to be my crew chief.

Guim said he understood the offer the previous year had been a bit low, then he went into a lot of detail about how Kawasaki worked with riders, supporting them medically, looking after any injuries, advising on nutrition. They wanted me fitness-tested and to check my blood levels to see what illnesses I might be susceptible to. The detail he was going into felt a bit intrusive.

I really didn't buy into it, because I'd never had a team looking after me in that way before. I thought, 'Surely it's just about riding a bike, isn't it?' But after having a good chat with Pere, I began to realise their philosophy was for the team to look after the rider as much as they looked after the machine.

Guim offered me a salary that was half the amount I was getting with Honda, but win bonuses were a little better. That seemed bizarre because the opportunities to win on the Kawasaki were so much better, but if I could put a season together like I was forecasting I might come out earning about the same.

I liked a lot about it, though. Yes, I would be taking on all the pressure that went with joining the number one guy at the time – Tom was still leading the championship back then. And it was clear I wouldn't be able to take Chris Pike with me. But it would be a system reboot, a refresh, new motivation and a serious possibility to win the World Superbike Championship.

Everything was on their terms, though, and I just wasn't relating to the main man Guim. Through all these early stages I was reaching out to Steve Guttridge, the racing manager of Kawasaki Europe, who I'd known since my early days in motocross and had become a close friend. I said to Steve, 'Guim is doing his best to fuck up this deal. He's not being very fast or flexible with things.'

But I didn't have any other choice if I wanted to win. So the only thing left to do was sign a letter of intent.

We went to round ten of the championship at Jerez, and the night before the race I crept off in the dark to the Kawasaki hotel on my little Honda Zoomer paddock scooter. It was a stone's throw from the paddock gates and I went into a room with Steve Guttridge, Guim and his brother Biel, who looks after the team's marketing and PR. I felt like I was on some kind of spy mission and we were all sworn to secrecy until the end of the season.

As I left with a signed letter of intent in my hand, I was immediately spotted by the Alpinestars Superbike manager. So it didn't stay a secret for very long, even though I couldn't talk about it.

I told Honda the following day in the office of the team's hospitality unit. I'd been talking to my crew chief Chris Pike about the Kawasaki deal all the way through, and he understood better than anyone why I needed to move on. The rest of the guys completely understood my motivations too and I think they were looking for a change as much as I was. They also had a bit of renewed enthusiasm because they were bringing on their home-grown Dutch World Supersport champion, Michael van der Mark. It turned out pretty well for them on the other side of the garage too, because they ended up signing Sylvain Guintoli.

A lot of people often ask if I regretted staying with Honda so long and I always answer, 'Not at all.' I worked with some amazing people and it prepared me for winning world championships. Some riders don't understand how good they've got it, until it's gone. I was kind of the other way around and spent a lot of years scraping for everything we could get.

At the end of my years with Honda I was always well paid, and they looked after me well with the Suzuka 8 Hours programmes. On the whole, it was a win-win situation: if I won on the bike, it was because of me as a rider, but if I didn't win, well, fourth or fifth was about where the bike deserved to be. I was super-proud I took the Fireblade to at least one race win in each of the six seasons I rode it, a total of 15. I never had any problems beating my team-mates, and we got through quite a few of those. It was often too comfortable a situation to leave, until finally the fire burned out and enough was enough.

I hated it when riders, journalists or even fans used the word 'factory' to describe the Honda. It gets used all over the place, like 'so-and-so is on a factory bike ...' For me, when you use that word, you're talking about a bike that is hand-built in a factory for one reason: to go racing. We never had that at Honda and never had any influence from HRC. In fact, HRC messed up more things at Ten Kate than they helped with.

We did the best we could with what we had, and when I signed off that 2014 season with an amazing second place at Qatar, I felt it was probably the best I'd ever ridden. I put my heart and soul into that race, because I wanted to tick a box that said, 'My job's done here. I've done the best I could for you guys.'

Since that point, they've never sniffed the top three in the championship.

It feels a bit weird walking past Ronald and the guys in the paddock now. I could have stayed and carried on earning decent money with good win bonuses because I was still winning now and again. It even made me a bit of a hero, because I was winning on the clear underdog.

People used to say I was a good rider and getting the best out of the Honda, but nobody actually knew what would happen when I left. I could have just been another fast guy, but I would never have known for certain until the moment I rode a proven bike, so it made leaving a really big decision.

I will always be grateful to people like Ronald and Robert Watherston, who, to this day, haven't given up hope of getting a bit of help from Honda in Japan. They still have faith in the project and in the Honda way. When Robert came to the project, I started to feel valued – he came from a Formula 1 background, and I suddenly got to fly business class because the culture there was to look after the rider. When I broke my femur in Germany, he and the team arranged for a private jet back to the Isle of Man because they knew Tatia was pregnant ... and they probably knew it would win them a brownie point or two when it came to renewing a contract for 2014.

But Robert had to go out and find money wherever he could to fund the Honda project with this private team, run out of a dealership in Holland and competing against Kawasaki, Aprilia and Ducati. People like him are the unsung heroes of the sport.

While I couldn't talk about the Kawasaki deal after Jerez, I gave Pere Riba the nod that we had got the deal done.

I swore him to secrecy too, but it didn't stop him immediately setting up a WhatsApp group with my other two mechanics, Uri and Arturo. We introduced ourselves and started chatting straight away, which swiftly broke the ice. It was like starting at a new school, so by the time we started working together officially, I felt like we knew each other well. Uri and Arturo even went to the effort of measuring the handlebar, seat and footpeg positions on my Honda in parc fermé at the final round in Qatar so they could replicate it in preparation for the winter tests. I remember being very proud of that last race with Honda and it got quite emotional with the team, but afterwards I trundled my kit bag from the Honda garage up to Kawasaki's because they would be sending it back to Europe with their equipment.

IN THE BEGINNING, I found it quite difficult working with Guim, because he never switches off. We would talk on the phone and he'd tell me I'd have an email by the end of the day. I might be hanging on, checking and re-checking my inbox until I went to bed, but then wake up the next morning to find the email had arrived at 1.00 in the morning!

It was such an exciting time for me, although I felt under so much pressure. This was the opportunity I'd been waiting for, and although the press and fans and people in the paddock had been so kind over the Honda years, telling me what a good rider I was, I honestly didn't know. I *couldn't* know how good I was until I rode a bike that was capable of winning the championship. So it was with huge nervous anticipation that I went to that first November test at a chilly Aragon circuit in Spain for my first ride on the Kawasaki ZX-10R.

It was certainly a proven bike. Tom Sykes had come within half a point of winning in 2012, before he won in 2013 – Kawasaki's first championship since Scott Russell 20 years before.

I'll never forget that day at Aragon. As I rode on my out lap there was a moment, between turn three to turn five – an uphill section comprising a fast right and two lefts – when the most massive smile formed on my face.

This, I knew right then, was the bike.

As each lap went by, I got faster and faster; the throttle response was instant, the power delivery was so precise, it was agile and so stable on the brakes. I could not believe I had been able to compete against it for the previous few years.

Pere was very methodical during the test and we finished fastest. And we were fastest at the next test. And the test after that.

In my mind, I was thanking the Kawasaki team and riders of the last few years for putting in the effort to build such a capable bike. Ever since Kawasaki had teamed up with the Provec team in 2012, it had been clear from the start that they had a pretty fast bike and were serious about their World Superbike programme.

At the last test at Jerez, Pere called it early as it was wet on the final day. We'd got through a lot of work and we were happy with our progress. I'd set the fastest wet time within six or seven laps and the forecast said it would carry on raining. So we packed up and I went back to the hotel with my assistant, Kev, while Tom stayed on a bit, pounding out some more laps. Later, we were in the bar, chilling with a beer, when Tom and his crew chief Marcel Duinker joined us. They started moaning about how hard it had been to win the championship in 2013 and how they'd just lost the 2014 championship in the final races. They were complaining about how bad the suspension was and that they'd set the bike up as well as they could.

I felt like getting them a box of tissues from my room and saying, 'Guys, dry your eyes. You've no idea how lucky you are on this package. I've just come from a private team who did their best on a hugely inferior bike to just get near the front. You've got the best bike in the paddock and you're moaning your tits off?!'

It was so funny, I was laughing to myself, because it was like they were beaten before we'd even started the 2015 season. I had come in with such a positive vibe and they were so down.

I didn't tell them that I'd known from those moments between turns three and five on that first out lap at Aragon that this bike could make my dream come true – that with this bike I could become world champion.

CHAPTER 13

THE GRASS IS GREENER

AFTER THOSE INCREDIBLE first tests with the ZX-10R and the Kawasaki team, I spent a very happy winter with Tatia and Jake in her home town of Cowes on Phillip Island, ahead of the start of the season there. When I first met her family, I was instantly accepted by her parents, John and Barb, her brother Jarv and his wife Kara and close family friend Kaye.

It's something we now do every year, because the weather's warm. I can do a lot of cycling with a group of cool guys I ride with regularly, and it's great for Tatia to spend time with her family after summer in the northern hemisphere. It's just the perfect environment in which to prepare for a new season, especially when the first round is just down the road.

In marrying Tatia, I found the Australian motorcycling community adopted me as a fellow Aussie, making Phillip Island feel like my 'real' home race. The support I get there is unbelievable and it's always an amazingly special and busy race for us with loads of family and friends.

Kawasaki hadn't ever won at Phillip Island and the target for me in the opening race of 2015 was clear. While some guys in the team were saying in the lead-up that the objective was a top five finish to put some points on the board, I was hell-bent on going out to try to win the race. I'd done a race simulation on the Friday and we knew we were critical on tyre wear, but I started from pole and I remember sitting on the grid, putting my brain where it needed to be and visualising this perfect start. My mechanics left the grid and told me everything was going to be great, but they reminded me to look after my tyre.

Phillip Island is unique among World Superbike circuits: quite a short start-finish straight, a couple of slower corners, but the rest of the track very fast, with high-speed turns which generally produce close races. It's an anti-clockwise track and its abrasive surface is very hard on the left side of the tyres, especially the long, last left-hand turn 12 on to the start-finish straight. The race can be won or lost in the final eight laps, so it's important to conserve some of the tyre for the last third of the race.

That day, some guys got quite excited in the early part of the race, like Michael van der Mark, who'd taken my ride at Honda. They wanted to go to the front and push on, but I knew I just had to stay in touch and keep my powder dry for the last four or five laps, riding quite conservative lines and not putting too much stress on the edge of the tyre. Towards the end, I felt the tyre was still there so I pushed the pace on a bit and, with Leon Haslam on his Aprilia and Ducati's Chaz Davies just behind, we built a bit of a gap to the second group. I knew Leon was sitting pretty and Phillip Island is one of his favourite tracks, but I put in an incredible last lap to get in front.

Crashing on oil at Nürburgring, 2013.
A split second later that left leg wasn't quite as straight.

Nice battle with Tom Sykes in Jerez, 2014. Ten months earlier I'd been developing new electronics, two seconds off the pace and trying to get a tow

Dear Ronald,

Thank you for giving me this
incredible opportunity to come
to the World Cha__ionship and for
continuing to believe in me,
all these years!!

I have had an amazing time
with the whole Ten Kate Honda team
which I'll never forget !!!

Thanks for the memories

JR

A special edition Arai with a thank-you note painted on the back for
my last race with Honda. I gave the helmet to Ronald.

Right: My first
dance with the
Ninja ZX-10R
Kawasaki at
Aragon Winter
Test 2014.

Left: I did plenty of
winning in 2015.
Here I am after
doing the double in
Misano with Kev.

Hanging out and riding with Jeremy 'Showtime' McGrath at Pala Raceway, California.

Winning my first World Championship in Jerez and thanking all the travelling support from Northern Ireland.

Left: Our first family photo with Tyler Jon Rea.

Left: Four weeks after giving birth, Tatia made me so proud by joining me at the FIM awards in Jerez to pick up my Gold medal.

Right: This was a promise between Jake and me. I'd told him before the weekend that if I did the double I'd take him on the podium.

Left: Off-season is as busy as during the season. Here at KHI in Japan with the race engineers talking about how we are going to improve.

Left: Celebrating our 2016 season with Guim Roda at a private party in Belfast.

Right: Last race of 2016 in Qatar playing the team-mate card. It didn't do me any favours.

Left: Our little piece of paradise in the Victorian mountains in Australia. Many off seasons have been spent suffering around here on my bicycle.

Right: My man cave at home is full of bikes. Of course, my favourite is the KX450 motocross bike.

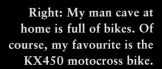

Left: Mixing business with pleasure. Taking a boat out to Phi Phi Islands, Thailand with my family after the opening race of 2017.

Right: There are worse ways to spend your fourth birthday. Heading to Magny-Cours to clinch the 2017 World Championship.

Left: Teaching Jake how to ride in the sand. Not sure Tatia loves the fact that he is so into bikes.

Right: One of my favourite photos ever. Can you imagine the motivation when you are not just winning for you?

Left: Lapping up the attention at Windsor Park before Northern Ireland's World Cup qualifier against Germany.

Right: Enjoying Las Vegas with Uri and Arturo after watching the Monster Energy Cup Supercross.

Left: Spending the summer with my family at our beach house on Phillip Island, Australia.

Right: After-party at SPOTY with Richard, his girlfriend Leanne, Tatia and my best mates Gav and Gaz.

Left: Picking up my MBE at Buckingham Place with Tatia, Mum and Dad.

Left:
The real
Team65.

Right: Pre-season MX camp.
I'd happily swap my three
World SBK Championships
for three World Motocross
Championships.

Left: Turn 11 at Brno,
Saturday 9 June 2018 –
the 2018 season got off
to a great start.

I knew that, even though we were down on power, our fourth gear was absolutely perfect for the last corner. As long as I could hold the outside line down the straight I would win, which is exactly what happened.

I crossed the line shaking my head in disbelief underneath the bubble of the screen. It was the perfect start to my partnership with Kawasaki. It was so cool for so many reasons – being part of the Phillip Island community during the off season, having Tatia's parents there who had never seen me win a race before, being the first guy to lead the world championship that year. It was an incredible feeling.

In race two, I got narrowly beaten on the line by Leon Haslam, making it a first and a second for both of us Honda refugees that day. I stood on the podium, watching a Honda technician walking back up the pit-lane from parc fermé, and for a second I felt a little bad about being there. But, I caught myself on, I shook my head and enjoyed the moment, and we had one hell of a party. In fact, we might actually have planted the seed of Tyler Jon Rea that night.

In the second round at Buriram in Thailand, a brand new circuit on the calendar, I went 1–1; I scored another 1–2 at Aragon, 1–1 in Assen, then another double at Imola. I couldn't believe what was happening and it seemed like our momentum was unstoppable.

I'd spent all winter trying to understand this new bike and it had taken a lot to adapt my riding style after so many years on the Honda. I didn't seem to be getting too much credit from the other side of the garage for my efforts, though.

In fact, Tom Sykes came out with the most incredible comment after those early races, saying the bike was built for me! He was effectively complaining that the ZX-10R suited my style more than his, but I'd been riding it for a few months, and this guy had been riding it since 2010. He'd won the championship on it and been runner-up twice. If it was made for one of the two of us, it certainly wasn't me. I had adapted to the bike, not the other way around.

Now we've been team-mates for a few years, I understand Tom's personality a little better. When he's being loud and crazy like that, I know how he's really feeling and I know he's one of these characters that has to say things out loud to convince himself that they're true.

Tom is very strange, a tight Yorkshireman. I've had loads of fun with that, like the time I suggested he and I split the whole bill in a flash restaurant on a team-building trip with the crew in Ibiza. His face almost fell off.

He's very guarded. I'd ask him how he is in the morning and he would just screw up his face and I'd see him thinking, 'Why's he asking me how I am? Should I answer honestly or throw a curve ball?' But he's not a bad person and has a good heart and decent morals and is devoted to his two daughters. We've had our run-ins, but I really respect his skills as a racer.

The other main contender that season, Chaz Davies, is very tall and lean, a square-jawed Welshman with a really dry and strange sense of humour. He can be very articulate but a little uptight and serious. From the outside, he seems a complex character with his own tight group of friends, but whenever we've had a few beers together, he still seems as guarded as when he's sober. I really respect him as a rider, though, and I see a bit of myself in Chaz.

In July we went to Laguna Seca in the USA and I finished third in both races, my worst results of the season so far – it sounds mad, even saying it now, but I had been either first or second in the 16 races up to that point.

There was some consolation after that relative disappointment. We flew to San Diego to ride with one of my all-time childhood heroes, motocross and supercross legend Jeremy McGrath, who had become a Kawasaki ambassador. All through the 1990s, while I was doing my schoolboy motocross, Jeremy was racking up titles in the American championships. I couldn't watch enough of his races.

We rode together at the famous Pala Raceway motocross track in the Californian desert between Los Angeles and San Diego to do some photos for Kawasaki and Monster Energy, who had arranged the day.

He was quite reserved in the beginning but super-cool and very laid-back in that typical Californian way, exactly how I thought he would be. I didn't want to creep him out by telling him how much I idolised him when I was younger – I've had that happen to me and it can be a bit weird. He said he was really into World Superbikes and MotoGP and asked me loads of questions about the championship. I was asking my own questions of him about riders he used to race against back in the day – guys like Jeff Emig, who I always loved to watch. We talked about how we were going to hit the jumps and I was so pumped when he said nice things about my motocross riding. They say never meet your heroes, but Jeremy was an exception. He just seemed like the kind of guy who, if I grew up racing with him, would be one of my mates. We got to swap helmets, as well, which was something really special, and he invited me out to ride at his ranch the next time I was back in the USA. I haven't had a chance to take him up on that yet, but one day ...

It was the ride of a lifetime and it inspired and motivated me to win race one at the next round in Sepang, in Malaysia.

Before race two, we worked out that if I won and Tom finished lower than fourth, I would win the championship before the six-week summer break.

I was having a real ding-dong battle with Chaz Davies on the last lap and, in typical Chaz fashion, he came down with a lunge into the last corner and rode us on to the big bump there, almost taking us both out. To be fair to Chaz, it was a championship-deciding race, so I would have done the same. He won and I was second, which I guess kept the organisers happy that the championship hadn't been decided so early in the season.

Tom had a problem in that race and finished something like 14th, but thank God I didn't win that time. It felt like nobody was ready for me to take the championship, including me. None of my family was there and I had a lot of racing left in the season and I probably would have switched off. All the same, I went into the summer break knowing I only needed six more points to make that long-held dream come true.

It was an incredible feeling and it should have meant I could relax and enjoy the break.

Not me though. I was actually so motivated that I trained harder than I ever had, riding my motocross bike heaps. I didn't let my hair down once – I'd got this close to fulfilling my dream, I didn't want to let it go now. I wanted to make sure there was nothing I'd left undone or unprepared, no reasons for failure, no excuses I could fall back on if I didn't get the job done.

Then, after this summer-long build-up that seemed to last forever, I went to Jerez in September and rode like a dick.

I didn't have a good feeling with the bike and I was just riding around like my head wasn't in it. In the first race, I wasted my tyre in the early laps and watched people riding away from me.

I finished fourth – and as I crossed the line I became world champion …

… which was so great, but … part of me felt crap! For the first time all season, I wasn't even on the podium.

I came back round to parc fermé and everyone was ecstatic. I was too, sort of. It was incredibly emotional. But I also felt I'd let myself down a bit, that I hadn't wanted to win it this way.

I'd spent a bit of time earlier that year on the Isle of Man with Neil Hodgson, who was telling me how he had won the 2003 championship with a whimper rather than a bang and that he would have given anything to have claimed his title with a race win.

Now I knew how he'd felt. I had to watch Tom, Chaz and Michael van der Mark celebrate on the podium while we had to focus on improving the bike for the next race.

And that made no difference either. I had another fourth, so still no fairy-tale finish. I know I work best when my back is against the wall, so maybe it was because all the pressure was off.

I watched another podium ceremony, then, as everyone drifted away back up the pit-lane, I got taken out on to the podium as a kind of afterthought for the photographs with my championship T-shirt and a small, token trophy. There were a few of my team down there with members of my family and the Superstock field just lining up on the grid for their race.

And that was it.

Twenty-two years of racing, from motocross through 125, Supersport and Superbike, in the UK and then all over the world. Twenty-two years of sacrifice and sometimes a lot of pain. Twenty-two years of seeing how championships were won in all kinds of racing, incredible euphoric climaxes with some of my all-time heroes, like that epic 2002 decider at Imola between Troy Bayliss and Colin Edwards. Finally, my Granda's prediction had come true.

Don't get me wrong. It was much better than not being champion. And, as any disappointment disappeared, that's what remained, and still remains today.

On the slow-down lap of that first race, I had looked up at my Granda and gave him a little wink. What you didn't see on the TV was all my family there, which meant so much, and the fact that Jerez had become a little corner of Northern Ireland, especially in the grandstand section at the end of the lap. There were huge numbers of travelling support for me, which was incredible. Of course, I wanted to celebrate with my wife and kids and family, who had sacrificed so much to get me there, but as soon as that was done I was flat-out busy with TV interviews, press conferences and photographs.

A bunch of aunts and uncles and a load of cousins came along with the rest of my family. Also there were Darren Roberts and Linda Pelham, who'd been through so much of the journey with me.

When I'd finished all my official media commitments, Stephen Watson and Gary McCutcheon from BBC Northern Ireland interviewed me outside the motorhome. Stephen has been a great support throughout my career, keeping my name on everybody's lips back home. He was the guy who had interviewed me back when I was 10 in the build-up to the weekend when I won the British championship. Here we both were, 18 years later, having an interview with me as world champion. The motorhome was parked about 75 metres from the bar underneath that main grandstand and our chat was drowned out by the sound of the Northern Ireland contingent singing the anthem of the rugby and football teams in the province, 'Stand Up For The Ulsterman'. I joked with Stephen, 'To be honest, I'd much rather be getting a few beers in with those boys!' But sadly, I had to keep my head relatively clear for a test scheduled the following day, which was all I needed to finish off my championship-winning weekend.

It wasn't until about 6.30 that night that I was actually able to get changed out of my team gear, sit down with that first beer and say to myself, 'Wow! I've actually just won the world championship.' But by that time, all the excitement and euphoria had actually gone – I was so tired.

After the test the next day, we went out for a team dinner and I had a few beers to relax. I ended up talking to one of my mechanics about the difficult relationship I'd had with Guim earlier in the season. I really started opening up about my feelings, but I woke the next morning with the horrors on because I remembered that his cousin, Alvar, was sitting with us and must have heard the whole conversation. I was thinking I'd better have a word with Guim before it all came out wrong, but I had to travel to Kawasaki's HQ in Amsterdam for a get-together, so that was going to have to wait.

Kawasaki Europe had prepared a big presentation and I got to meet a lot of the staff there. They'd also arranged a small celebration which I think I would have enjoyed a little more if Tatia hadn't been so heavily pregnant with Tyler. We were also with Jake, who was two, and it all got a little scratchy because we were all quite tired.

But slowly I started to realise that, as far as Kawasaki was concerned now, I was *the* guy. They didn't have a MotoGP team to help market their products, so World Superbikes was the pinnacle of their motorsport programme, and it didn't get better than winning the world championship. It wasn't a question of going to a local dealer down the road to sign a few autographs and get a few selfies taken; it was a full-on Asian tour at the end of that season.

Before that, I got back to winning ways with a double at Magny-Cours in France and a final podium in race one at Qatar, although I finished the very last race with a technical problem. By that time all the feelings of euphoria and satisfaction had worn off, because I'd won the championship so early. But part of that Asian tour was helping to promote a new ZX-10R for 2016 that Kawasaki had launched, so understanding their continuing commitment to the programme was great motivation as we headed towards another winter testing programme.

It had turned into an incredible year and my move to Kawasaki had been totally vindicated. The only thing I still needed to understand a little better was my relationship with Guim.

As I've gone through life, I've met people I've really respected, and I have immediately wanted those people to like me and respect me back. Of course, I've met plenty of total assholes too, and not given a thought to what they think! Guim was a person I respected and who I felt I needed to impress, but in 2015 I never got that arm around the shoulder from him, no pat on the back that I need from time to time. It's almost like I was a dog and Guim was my owner, and I wanted to please him and to see that he was pleased.

Back when I saw that Honda technician walking past the podium on Phillip Island, I was actually looking for Guim because I couldn't see him celebrating my victory with the rest of the team. It was my first race for Kawasaki, my first win, and his absence pissed me off a bit.

I was the new boy on the team, that was fine, and I understood Tom Sykes was the number one, having been world champion and runner-up twice, but I was kind of looking for the team manager to be showing a little appreciation of my first win. It wasn't until November that I managed to find the guts – backed up, of course, by a world championship – to have a conversation with him about how I had been feeling.

It turned out the reason Guim wasn't under the podium was because he was in the garage drying Tom's tears and encouraging him after he'd had a really tough race. And it had become evident as the season progressed that Tom needed more of the babysitting, while I was more self-sufficient. I completely see now that this is the manager in Guim and he was doing what was needed to get the best out of his rider. He's done exactly the same with me, whenever I've had an issue.

Guim and I got our relationship sorted and, together with my team, we had the 2015 championship sorted too. We turned into a winning machine and I ended up with 14 wins that year. In all my six years with Honda, I had won 15.

The final thing to make the year complete was the birth of a little brother for Jake. Tyler Rea said hello to the world a few days after I got home from that final race of the season in Qatar. Tatia had an elective caesarean because of a few issues she had when giving birth to Jake, but thankfully it was all fairly straightforward in the end.

I wasn't sure I'd ever been happier in my life. I had my dream, my world championship and this perfect little family. But we certainly weren't prepared for what was coming next.

CHAPTER 14

BACK TO BACK

AS WE WENT into the winter of 2015–16, the reality of what I had achieved and how I had done it finally sunk in, but the emotion was quickly parked to make way for Tyler. We needed to make a lot of room for him, too, because while Jake had been an almost perfect baby, second time around Tatia gave birth to a little terror! The birth went smoothly enough, but soon afterwards we knew our lives were changing quite dramatically and the achievements of 2015 were already becoming a distant memory.

As I write this, Tyler is coming up to three and we couldn't be more proud of the little bruiser he has become. He's grown into a proper tough nut, bossing his big brother around and not being afraid to push the odd big kid around in the playground, too. This lad doesn't take any shit, even from me, and he shows no fear in anything. He's got a temper on him like his grandfather (the Aussie one), which sometimes isn't pretty. But he's super cute, funny and has a very big personality. Watch this space for young Tyler Jon. My mum tells me that he's exactly like I was as a toddler – full throttle – and it's going to be a very interesting journey to see what sort of adult he evolves into.

Tyler was the most difficult baby you could imagine – he didn't sleep, he was constantly sick, vomiting after every feed, and we eventually discovered he had a problem called silent reflux, which is extremely painful for babies. Acid from his stomach was coming up and irritating his oesophagus and throat, but he obviously had no way of telling us about this problem, other than screaming. Constantly.

When we finally had him diagnosed and were able to give him some medication to stop the burning pain, our lives started to turn for the better, but that was eight months into his life and halfway through the 2016 championship and the defence of my World Superbike title. It was a tough off-season, and preparation for the new season was difficult because I was away a lot with Kawasaki trying to maximise the return on their investment. I was sent to trade fairs all over the world to promote the new ZX-10R and went to Japan with Pere to attend meetings, celebration parties and even some wind-tunnel testing.

Luckily, our family of four was back to Australia in the New Year, which allowed me to switch off a bit so I could dedicate some time to being a dad and helping with the kids. Because it's in a different time zone, you're effectively out of reach and you can elect to delay responding to emails or text messages, which helped us a lot. But things got busy again with the press launch of the new bike at Sepang in early 2016. I went along for a few days and it was a good opportunity to get a feel for the base level of what I would be riding in 2016.

The new bike was a bit of an animal compared to the old model, having been developed mostly working with Tom and Loris Baz between 2012 and 2014, and had gone in the direction Tom had led the engineers. It required a unique style of late, late braking and hard acceleration, which was something I hadn't had to use before, and was something that followed more of Tom's natural riding style.

Pre-season testing in Spain went deceptively well, albeit in perfect conditions with quite high grip levels, which you can often expect in a cold European winter.

But while all my rivals were bigging themselves up on social media, saying how this was their year and all the usual stuff, at times I felt the least prepared I'd ever been.

Because of the issues with Tyler, it felt like I'd hardly slept that winter and, although I was training my ass off, it was like guilt training. I would jump from playing dad to throwing myself into training probably more than I should. In reality, I think I needed a bit more time to relax and recover, because playing dad felt physically and mentally draining enough.

It was hard on all of us but that purely selfish me, the focused and single-minded rider, still needed Tatia's emotional support, and if she was at breaking point she did her best to hide it.

On the Wednesday before the first round, we got her parents to look after the kids and drove into Cowes to get an ice cream together. I remember breaking down in tears to her, asking how the hell I was going to win a championship that year with what was going on at home, plus a new bike that I didn't have such a good feeling with. She basically told me to grow a set of balls and that it wasn't my job to break down over the problems we were having with Tyler – that was her job! She said I needed to wind my neck in, to stop feeling sorry for myself and to get on with riding the bike like the World Champion that I was.

It must have worked, because we hit the ground running with a double at Phillip Island and we went 1–2 with Tom in Thailand, getting the season off to an almost perfect start.

Also, I knew I wasn't feeling totally comfortable with the bike. So together with Pere, we explored all kinds of geometry and set-ups during the season and we altered the engine character quite a lot. Unlike the start of 2015, when I was so confident, it actually felt like the title might not be mine to win second time around, so I started exploring what else I could put in place to give me any extra advantage. One of those was to expand Team65 to include my good friend Fabien Foret, whose job would be to analyse all aspects of my riding to see where it might improve. So I had my crew chief Pere to look after the bike and now Fab to look after the rider.

I'd known Fab from racing. His partner, Emily, is Australian, and like me he spends a lot of the summer around Melbourne. Tatia and I rented an apartment with them in St Kilda during the Australian summer of 2012–13. Fab and I have done a lot of cycling together and the girls get on very well.

By 2016, Fab was coming towards the end of his riding career and was considering retirement, except for a select number of Endurance World Championship races. With his schedule freed up, I asked him if he'd consider working with me on a more professional level.

I was aware I had a very 'old school', upright riding style, kind of smooth yet aggressive, and there were areas that, with Fab's help, I wanted to improve. I'd seen younger riders dragging their elbows as well as their knees over the kerbs, hanging their heads way off the bike to maintain a low centre of gravity. I was riding a lot more with my legs and feet, rather than man-handling the bike with my arms, which probably harked back to my motocross days. So Fab began to act as my 'spotter' at various places around the track, taking notice of my style and where I could improve.

At the end of a session, he will tell me things like, 'Stop stressing with the bike, you're not even pushing – you're just cruising.' I might argue and disagree with him, telling him I'm riding hard, but standing at the side of the track he can use his racer's eye to tell whether I am or not. It's something I never got from Dad back in the early days, but Fab won't hold back, even though it might be difficult for me to hear at times. He's become more of a mentor for me, and he analyses each session so we can understand our rivals better and formulate strategies for the races.

With all the media commitments now and with the family in the paddock as well, it's great to have Fab there as someone whose judgement I can trust. He does a lot of the groundwork for me that otherwise I just wouldn't have time to do. He even has video programmes where he can super-impose footage of me on top of another rider to compare styles and racing lines. He also works closely with Pere and will look at particular sectors on a track where I might be losing a couple of tenths to my rivals. He's become a huge part of the team and I love making him proud of my riding and my results.

I'm lucky that I've earned enough to be able to invest in a lot of different ways to help me develop as a rider and concentrate on my job. That covers my management at International Racers and my full-time assistant Kev, who looks after everything – all my kit, nutrition, sponsor liaison, schedule – during a busy race weekend, drives our motor-home and stocks it with everything we need when we arrive. It sometimes feels like we've built a bit of a machine. I feel I can justify the expense with the win-bonuses I earn from being a better rider. Not many riders have riding coaches, or even assistants, and it's a huge investment, but I love an easy life and I really trust people unless they give me a reason not to. All these people around me who don't need micro-managing just make my life easier and allow me to get on with the job and have a relatively normal life when I'm away from the track.

When we got to the first European round at Aragon we realised we were struggling a bit – what seemed to have worked during our winter test there, with low temperatures and a lot of rubber on the circuit, suddenly wasn't working when the grip was reduced with higher track temperatures. The bike felt very different – I couldn't ride it how I wanted to, and I was still having to change my own style a lot.

From that point in the season, we adopted a strategy where, if we thought we could win we tried to make it count, but when we knew we couldn't, we just tried to be as good as we could be.

I knew that one place I could deliver was at Assen and we completed a really satisfying double there. Then it was a question of taking seconds and thirds where we could until Misano, always a favourite, for another double. We got to Laguna Seca in America and, although I won the first race there, I broke down in race two and had to retire. The following weekend we returned to the Lausitzring in Germany and I had another technical problem with the gearbox and ended up crashing. I'd found a false neutral and then rammed it into first gear before getting catapulted into the ground. Suddenly a 71-point lead in the championship after race one at Laguna – the equivalent to almost three race wins – had been reduced to a 26-point advantage over Tom with seven races left. It was the slimmest margin I'd had since after the first few races of 2015.

I thought there were two ways to manage it. I could ride defensively, picking up podiums and wins where possible to maintain the gap; or I could come out fighting and be really positive. We woke up on the Sunday morning for race two to the sound of rain hammering down on the roof of the motorhome and, as any race fan will tell you, when the rain comes you double the risk of making a mistake. Race two conditions were going to be very slippery, with everyone riding on a knife edge, tiptoeing around and trying to find grip in the horrendous conditions.

Only I didn't see it like that. I saw the rain as my chance to win and get my championship back on course.

I had a pretty bad qualifying session and was starting from sixth. I got my head down from the first lap, found my way to the front quite early and, from then on, just kept on increasing the gap. I won by 14 seconds.

That feeling was amazing, and I think it goes down as one of the most important and satisfying race wins in my Superbike career. I felt like I'd been pushed into a corner and had to come out fighting. I've had the feeling at various moments throughout my career, but I don't think I've ever felt it more than that day in Germany. The confidence it gave me was incredible, because I was able to turn the potential adversity into such a positive feeling and a significant result. It was a vital win and an impressive way to do it when our backs were really against the wall. I remember that Sunday night as one of the best we've ever had in the motorhome, with a few glasses of wine and the belief that we'd got things back on track.

I think before that race both my main rivals, Tom and Chaz Davies, thought they could get the championship done because the momentum had been with them.

The problem with the gearbox that I'd had in Laguna and Lausiztring had actually been recurring throughout the season. The more we worked on improving it, the further we got away from a good base setting. It got to the point where we were changing electronics strategies as well as physical parts to try to give me a better feeling. With this sort of trial and error approach, I ended up making mistakes in the most stressful moments, when you needed a gear to engage and it wouldn't. That was the issue in my crash at Lausitzring and it also cost me a race win at Donington.

It all frustrated me a lot and took away a lot of focus on other key areas during the year, but we still maintained the step-by-step philosophy that we applied in 2015. By the end of the season, it was new territory for me heading into the last round and still needing to win the championship. But we were able to get the job done and secure the title in the first race under the floodlights at Qatar. It was great and it honestly felt even better than winning the previous year.

Even though I didn't win that race, at least I managed to get on the podium, so it was an improvement on Jerez in 2015. But there were no spectators in Qatar; it still felt really strange and a little empty. This time, though, I understood much better what it meant to win the championship, that it wasn't just about one moment you had dreamed about all your life. We had won nine races, but it had been an extremely challenging year. We really struggled at some circuits, but still managed to get it done.

It made me realise how much more satisfying it was when you have to dig deeper as a team to overcome issues and get the results. I remember Pere laughing and saying to me in parc fermé, 'We fucking won this championship with a blunt knife!'

Race two in Qatar had its own particular interest, even though the first race had settled the championship.

That season honestly could have belonged to Chaz had he not made so many mistakes. He won a total of 11 races to my nine, but on a few occasions when he should have just finished the race he would inexplicably end up in the gravel. He was out of the hunt for the title, but he still had a chance to beat Tom for second. He'd won six of the previous seven races and had dominated the last part of the season. Guim came to me during the afternoon build-up to the night race and we talked about the points situation with Tom and Chaz. I could see what was coming to be honest, and he explained about the value to Kawasaki of having a 1–2 in the championship, and the monetary value to the team as well. He sold me the idea of helping Tom if I could.

I'm not completely proud of agreeing to the plan, or what happened in the race that night to make the plan come to fruition, but I understand that's how motorsport works sometimes. The fact is Chaz deserved to finish second that year and, if he hadn't made so many mistakes, he could have been fighting for the championship as he put a much better season together than Tom. I felt bad because I was the guy that took second place away from him.

Also, Tom and I didn't have the closest of relationships and part of me felt like I was giving this guy something he didn't really deserve. He had seemingly questioned where I was taking the development of the bike and a lot of things that Pere or myself would say. Tom always talked a lot about preferring a bike with light inertia, which suited his riding style. It allowed him to brake deeper into a corner, square it off into a V-shape by apexing earlier and getting the bike upright quickly to accelerate out again. The more conventional style would be to open up the corner with a more sweeping line to carry a higher speed around the apex.

With the old championship regulations, you used to be able to lighten the bike's crankshaft which helped him a lot with that. Although that was banned in 2015, Kawasaki still developed the 2016 bike with Tom in mind, with a lighter crank as standard. In theory, the bike would stop and accelerate faster but be a little more aggressive on the power. My natural flowing style prefers the opposite – something that's slightly less reactive. But, instead of understanding that different things worked for each of us, Tom got his back up a bit and insisted the bike that suited his style was the right way to go. His attitude was, 'I've taken Kawasaki from nothing to winning a world championship. I've led the development of the bike and I know what I'm talking about.' The implication was always that what I wanted was wrong. It was ironic that the 2016 bike had the decreased inertia that he wanted, but in every post-race comment he would talk about inertia and the limitations he was facing.

So there was a lot of conflict going on in my head and it made me think I just wanted to win that second race in Qatar and let Tom and Chaz fight over who was going to finish second and third in the championship. I got a great start in the race but began to go backwards because it felt like there was an electronics problem cutting the power. As it turned out, the race was red flagged and when I returned to the garage my mechanics quickly spotted a sensor problem and fixed it; but I had dropped to ninth place before the red flags came out, so that's where I had to line up on the grid for the restart.

I'll never forget the next 10 laps, which were just about the most amazing laps of my life. I broke the lap record three laps in a row and got up to second to start chasing down Chaz, who had built a big lead. I had just reached him going on to the last lap and the gap was three-tenths of a second, but I'd been so focused on chasing him that I hadn't thought about where I was going to pass him. I realised it was probably not going to be possible and not worth the risk of a big lunge, so I completely backed out of it and played the team card that we had discussed before the race.

I was so proud of the way I had raced. I rode like an animal, coming from ninth on the grid. Tom seemed happy that he had just been gifted second place in the championship, but, apart from a gesture of thanks on the slow-down lap, there wasn't much else from him. I think he acknowledged something for the TV cameras, but we didn't discuss it at any point afterwards, even though the move had probably taken a huge amount of money away from Chaz in the form of bonuses and gifted it to Tom.

Maybe my expectations were a bit too high, but I can only imagine if someone had put me in that position, I would have sent them something very special by way of thanks and to acknowledge what had happened.

If Chaz had been my team-mate I would have done it for him, and he and I didn't discuss it afterwards. I'm sure he would have seen it coming and he would have done the same thing if he'd been in my position. But the way Tom was afterwards, and how he spoke about me as a team-mate going into the off-season, helped make up my mind that I would never do it again.

I don't have a huge rivalry with any of these guys, although something has been built from the outset about my battles with Chaz – different manufacturers, green against red, and everything. But I think that episode kick-started a huge fire in him to beat me that would erupt in a volcano in 2017.

From a racing point of view, 2016 was hard, as I never felt that comfortable with the bike and with the technical issues we had. The 2015 bike had been developed over many, many years and was the finished package when I joined Kawasaki, whereas the 2016 version was an all-new model, with some of the niggles and teething problems you'd expect. So I was really proud of winning back-to-back championships like Fred Merkel, Doug Polen and Carl Fogarty. Winning my second championship on a new model made it feel really, really special.

Back-to-back titles was a pretty big deal and had only been done those three times, but even though the championship went down to the last round, I'd been planning during the final few races to hold a championship party in Northern Ireland for about 200 people.

It was incredible to spend the night with so many friends and family, and we had top Irish radio DJ Pete Snodden and X Factor finalist Simon Lynch to sing live. We'd never really had a chance to celebrate 2015 properly, because I'd parked the emotion to concentrate on more important things like becoming a dad for the second time. So Tatia and I planned this double celebration with everyone who had played a part in both championships and we got the crew over from Barcelona, which was really cool.

Almost as soon as we'd polished up the hangovers, though, we headed to Australia to rest, relax and be a family that stayed in one place for more than a week at a time. Along with my motocross camp in Spain at the beginning of a new season, the winter in Phillip Island has become a key ritual now – there are no distractions, life is normal, I go pretty much unnoticed and we have some good family downtime. I celebrated hard at the end of the 2016 season, so it was time try to shed those extra few kilos, put in some hard training to prepare fully for 2017 and see if I could be the first champion ever to make it three in a row.

CHAPTER 15

MAKING A POINT

I KNOW HOW hard our life is on Tatia, because the schedule puts so much pressure on her with the boys. I know kids like routines, and ours are dragged through airports every couple of weeks, sleeping in different beds. It's not real life – and I'm not saying this for any kind of sympathy – but I feel like I put my family through a washing machine sometimes, just getting to a race. That's fine while you have energy to do it, but when she's wrung out, the whole thing can wobble a bit and then I might start to wobble.

So it's become important for me to work on keeping her spirits up, keeping her positive. We've been bringing up our two boys on the Isle of Man with no real support network of family, babysitters or childcare, so when I'm around I try to play 'Dad' the best I can. I really love cooking, so as well as getting meals ready for the boys, I like to surprise Tatia sometimes with a gastronomic masterpiece. I'm lucky enough to have travelled all over the world and sampled some amazing cuisines, some of which I have a go at replicating in my own kitchen. I'd really love to have go on *Masterchef* one day. As for a favourite dish, it's difficult to beat a few really nice rib-eye steaks on the barbeque with some mashed potato and vegetables.

But when I'm away sometimes at flyaway races on my own, Tatia has to manage it all herself. So, as nice as life on the road can seem to be, it is tough at times. I invest a lot in making things as comfortable as they can be – we'll often stay in an airport hotel rather than get a really early or late flight and, when we're racing in Europe, we're lucky to live in a nice motorhome. While I know money can't buy happiness, it can make life on the road easier sometimes.

The rewards of travelling with the family are huge. It's great to come home and look through pictures of Tatia and the boys celebrating with me and the rest of the team in parc fermé, or getting the boys up on the podium. The memories we're building now will be with us forever. We only get one shot at this life, and I think we're doing our best as a family to make the most of the opportunities we've been given.

Tatia is such great fun to be around; she's the person everyone wants to come and have a party with. Her biggest quality is she puts every other person before herself. She has a wide network of friends and, while I know I only see it from my point of view, I think she's probably a much better friend to them than they are to her. She also applies her selflessness to me and the kids and she's the best mum you could imagine. We often joke that while my job provides the incredibly privileged life we lead as a family, she's the one that creates everything we do and the adventures that we all enjoy.

They understand now at Kawasaki that she's a huge part of the Team65 machine, even though she's happy to stay in the background. She's not employed by them but she's there, and Pere will often speak with her about what's going on in my head, so he can try to get the best from me.

It can be difficult and stressful sometimes with all the PR and marketing commitments that go with the job now, and they can pull the family all over the place. I am too selfish and I need her there too much to say to Tatia, 'Look, this is my thing, my job, you stay home, be a mum, and I'll take care of everything.' My travel expenses for each race are probably quadruple those of other riders, because there are four of us on the road now and I want to keep that family unit together because it means so much to me.

AFTER RESTING AND getting back into good shape physically in Australia over the European winter, it was time for us all to get back to it. Our pre-season testing for 2017 went really well. Pere understood the mistakes that had been made with the bike in 2016 and he knew what changes were needed to make it better.

But the season might easily have been over before it began after a little incident at turn three at Jerez during winter testing.

I was coming out of turn two in first gear and 'short-shifting' – changing up a gear earlier at lower RPM – from second to third. There was a kind of delay in the gears engaging that created a spike in the revs. When they did engage a fraction of a second later, I had a huge highside and barrel-rolled across the gravel. I was a little groggy and winded when I got to my feet. It was more of a freak incident and nothing to do with the issues we'd had the previous year. Maybe my foot hovered too long on the lever.

As the marshals helped me off to the side of the track, I could see the bike was in bits. They made me go straight to the medical centre where I peeled off my leathers for a check-up, but everything was OK.

It was one of the biggest crashes I'd had in recent years. I knocked myself around quite a bit, but amazingly I got up, walked away and had no injury. I put that down to the airbag built into my Alpinestars Tech-Air suit, which is pretty much like an inflatable life vest that fits inside my leathers. It has very clever sensors that detect unexpected gyroscopic forces and basically forecast when you're going to crash. The airbag inflates in 25 milliseconds – about 15 times faster than you can blink – and protects virtually the entire torso. It's prevented injury in a lot of crashes I've had that a few years ago would have really messed up a season. The kind of technology we're lucky enough to have in racing now – along with traction control and other aids – is prolonging careers.

In Jerez, I simply dusted myself down, got changed, went to grab some lunch and when I got back on the bike in the afternoon, I went even faster.

After the challenges of 2016, Pere was reinventing the base set-up of the bike and I was already developing a very special relationship with the 2017 version.

The season started incredibly well with a double at Phillip Island, and we followed that with another double in Thailand. When we got to Aragon, I was involved in two epic battles with Chaz which came down to last lap deciders. He made a mistake in race one and went down in the last corner, but in race two he just came out on top.

During qualifying at the next race at Assen, my relationship with Chaz took a bit of a hit. Whether I like it or not, he had been my main rival since I first moved to Kawasaki, consistently the strongest competitor, and we had enjoyed a lot of close battles together.

I had completed my Superpole lap in qualifying, probably the most perfect lap I'd ever done around Assen and a pole position lap time that will likely stand for a few years to come. Chaz was making a second attempt at a fast lap.

I'd rolled off the gas going through a fast section on the back part of the circuit, when I saw someone was coming, I didn't know who, and I got off-line ... but I clearly didn't move off enough and I ended up in his way on a corner exit. It was Chaz and as he passed me, he reached over and hit me with his fist, followed by a load of distinctly unfriendly hand signals.

Back at parc fermé, he called me a 'fucking prick' and was saying all kinds of ridiculous things in front of the TV cameras, trying to make me out like a real villain.

I stayed quite calm when he was giving it the big one. To be honest, part of me quite enjoyed watching him make a fool of himself. At that point, I hadn't seen any footage and felt I was pretty much off the racing line, but I realised I'd done something to upset him and thought maybe I was in the wrong.

I wasn't intentionally trying to hold up anyone, because no-one was going to beat me that day. On top of that, I had only dropped five points in the first six races of the season with that second place in Aragon, and I guess Assen was looking like another demolition job.

However, I was summoned to the headmaster's office in race control and, whether they felt it was fair or not, I think they believed they had no alternative but to penalise me in some way. Chaz and Ducati were clutching at straws and demanding some kind of sanction. I watched the footage and stood my ground as best I could, saying that, while I agreed I had got in his way, I'd given him plenty of space and it was him that was off-line. He'd missed his apex by a country mile, which sent him out wide, and if he'd been on a normal line he wouldn't have come anywhere near me.

In the end though, they dropped me three grid places. After the best Assen lap of my life, I wasn't going to be allowed to start from pole position.

Talk about red rag to a bull.

I started from fourth on the grid in race one and ninth in race two, but there was no way I was going to get beaten in either and we scored another double. I was so fired up.

What happened after the races definitely wasn't cool and fired me up even more. In a statement on Facebook, Chaz said, 'If you get your kicks from putting other riders' lives in danger, good for you …

'… he knew I was coming and endangered both of us with his underhand games.

'I'd expect fairer play from a novice, let alone a double World Champion.'

From the mentions I was receiving, I could see he'd been getting a bit of negative reaction on social media for acting like a spoiled brat in parc fermé. There were suggestions he was trying to manipulate the situation by implying I had form for this kind of riding. I lost a lot of respect for Chaz and his bully-boy tactics when I read that. The Kawasaki team's PR chief Biel Roda asked me if I wanted to counter with something but I said no, not at all. I think clever people understood what was happening and I quickly moved on.

While I believe Chaz is quite intelligent, I certainly don't believe he wrote those social-media posts. We'd never had a problem before, other than our ongoing rivalry, but I could always tell from Chaz's facial expressions how seriously he took himself. He's a strange character and because he was my closest rival, the next few races were tough. We share the same space a lot of the time – we're in parc fermé together, behind the podium, on the podium, in press conferences, in safety commission meetings. There was definitely a big elephant in the room when we were together.

Anyway, after Assen the season was starting to feel even better than 2015, like a diesel train that wasn't slowing down.

We got beaten by Chaz in the next round at Imola; he was riding very well and the track suited the Ducati a little better. Then we went to Donington, where Tom had been unbeaten for something like four years. Like Aragon had been to Chaz and Assen to me, it was Tom's happy hunting ground. Breaking his domination was a particularly special motivation.

The weekend went pretty well and I was leading Tom by around two seconds in race one, when I got a little vibration from my rear wheel. I thought the tyre might have spun on the rim and become unbalanced, which can happen sometimes, so I backed right off and was forced to let Tom come past.

I was just trying to nurse the bike home but, as I came down the hill at Craner Curves, through the fast fourth-gear left-hander, it felt like someone in the crowd had shot my rear tyre away with a sniper rifle.

I had a massive highside and went spinning into the gravel. I was pretty beaten up but again was saved from serious injury and was ready for race two thanks to my Arai helmet and that Alpinestars suit.

For reasons we didn't really understand, the tyre had just exploded and come off the rim. The same thing happened to Michael van der Mark when he was leading at the next race in Misano. Pirelli had said they were developing new compounds and constructions and sometimes you go down a wrong path in development and make mistakes. We went back to a tried and trusted construction without any further issues, while Pirelli removed that particular tyre from the allocation for safety reasons.

So after losing out on a lead in race one, I had an even bigger motivation to go out and do what I could to win race two.

We were pretty relaxed and joking beforehand and Uri, my chief mechanic, begged me to go out and beat Tom and underline it with a big wheelie across the line. It was going to be a huge ask, because of the reverse-grid rule for race two that the organisers had introduced for 2017. Because I didn't finish race one, I had to start from tenth place, on the fourth row, but I had a fantastic start and rode an amazing first lap; by turn one on the second lap I was leading, and I tried to manage the race from there. Tom started from ninth on the grid and eventually fought his way up to second. With a few laps to go, I had a comfortable enough gap but not enough to do a proper celebration, so I really dug in to open it up a bit.

It worked, and I crossed the line with a stand-up wheelie for Uri! It was so nice to win at a circuit I'd always struggled at. It was also great for me to take Kawasaki's 100th World Superbike victory, which the whole team was able to celebrate in parc fermé and on the podium with the 1–2 we got in the race.

The following race at Misano was less of a triumph. When Michael van der Mark's rear tyre went, I was right behind him and had to go off the track to avoid hitting him, which allowed Chaz to go in front.

I hauled him back and was mounting a challenge on the last lap when Chaz tucked the front and crashed in front of me with two corners left.

I had nowhere to go and rode over the top of him.

I came off too. The first thing I thought about, just for a moment – my racer's brain kicking in again – was my race.

'Fuck, he's taken the race away from me!' Then I realised I'd hit Chaz badly. It was horrible and thoughts started rushing through my head about Marco Simoncelli, a really talented and popular MotoGP rider, who was killed in a similar accident at Sepang in Malaysia in 2011.

However, as I got up and instinctively ran to pick up my bike, I glanced back and saw Chaz getting up like some kind of superhero and trying to lift his own bike.

I thought, 'Shit, I've got to beat him to the line!' I got back on my bike, which was quite badly damaged, and completed the next two corners. I actually finished third, because Chaz and I had been so far ahead.

On the slow-down lap, I was thinking about Chaz and wondering if he was OK or whether he'd actually finished the race. I'd seen him get up with my own eyes, but when I got to the corner where we had crashed I saw his bike leaning against the tyre wall. Some paramedics looked like they were still treating him, so I ran over to see how he was. I remember holding his head like I was some kind of medical expert, reassuring him that he was going to be OK. When I finally got to the podium, I was in no mood to celebrate with my team-mate, who had won the race by picking up the pieces of the carnage that had happened in front of him.

As soon as the ceremony was finished and I'd done the media interviews, I got changed and went up to the medical centre on my scooter and hung around outside with Ducati team manager Serafino Foti, waiting for news. I had run over Chaz's torso and upper arms and he was later diagnosed as having fractured a vertebra. I didn't leave until I heard he was stable. I kept going over the crash in my mind, because it was so similar to Simoncelli's and also the one that killed Craig Jones at Brands Hatch in 2008. It brought it home in my mind again that anything can happen.

When the championship rocked up at Laguna Seca three weeks later, Chaz had made this miraculous comeback and even won race one. Thankfully, I followed up by winning race two.

I'd sent him a message after Misano saying I hoped he wasn't too beaten up. But we didn't really get a chance to talk until I bumped into him in a bar on the Sunday night at Laguna Seca, and I think he'd probably had a couple of beers. We started talking and, although we didn't actually mention our row at Assen, I did open up a bit about how bad I felt about the way 2016 had ended with Tom and the team orders. I think it probably went in one ear and out the other, but I was glad to have got that bit of our story out in the open, because Chaz definitely deserved to be second that year.

THAT TOOK US into a shorter summer break which allowed me to spend a few weeks at home on the Isle of Man, recharge the batteries and get motivated for a strong end to the season.

Instead of thinking about winning the championship, I was more focused on the last two rounds of the season at Jerez and Qatar, because they were circuits where I'd never won.

But before those challenges, we went to Lausitzring for the next round, a track we had struggled at before because the layout didn't really suit the character of our bike. Sure enough, we couldn't match Chaz's pace and he won both races. But even on bad days like those, it seemed we were still able to mix it at the front and we went 2–2.

Before the championship returned to the Portimao circuit in Portugal for the first time in a couple of years, Tatia and I took the boys for a little holiday at an all-inclusive resort on the Algarve. It was the first time the four of us had been away as a family unit and we spent the week on the beaches, having a proper bucket and spade holiday. It was bliss hanging out with the kids all morning in the pools and, when they went for their naps in the afternoon, I'd go running up and down the most beautiful beaches.

At the track, from the start of free practice we had an awesome weekend and I took pole position and both race wins. My championship position was further strengthened by Tom having a huge crash on one of the steep downhill sections in FP3 and having to sit out the weekend with a badly broken little finger.

All of a sudden, a slim championship lead had turned into a procession and we were able to start planning some celebrations for after Magny-Cours, where it seemed all I had to do was finish upright and we would get the job done. With that in mind, I set about making arrangements to get back to Belfast on the Sunday night after hopefully winning the championship. I thought it would be great to have a bit of a get-together at the airport and a party with some of my friends to celebrate.

A few weeks before, I had got in touch with an old friend, Joanne McNeill, who I knew from my early days with Red Bull. She worked in PR and marketing and I told her I was needing some help with personal media commitments, especially at home in Northern Ireland, now that I had some titles under my belt. Joanne had some very good contacts and started working with me from the middle of 2017, arranging all my personal PR. She told me there would probably be a few people waiting for the plane to welcome me home, with maybe some press and interviews to be done.

We splashed out and booked a private jet both ways, because Magny-Cours is in the middle of nowhere and can be a pain with flights to Paris and a three-hour drive from the airport. But we also had a bit of an entourage that weekend; along with my mum and my brother we had a TV crew, plus my friend and video producer Gaz Price, and Stephen Watson and Gary McCutcheon from BBC Northern Ireland. Stephen and Gary were planning a documentary on my season, because of the possibility of me becoming the first World Superbike rider to win three championships in a row.

The trip didn't get off to the best of starts because the aircraft we booked had a technical problem, so they had to send another, which made us late for some PR commitments in Paris with Eurosport. But it was also Jake's birthday and the plane's crew had arranged a cake. After that quick Parisian pit-stop, we climbed back on board for the short flight down to Nevers and then on to the Magny-Cours circuit, where the team had laid on a special birthday dinner with balloons and hats. It was all really nice and actually helped me a lot, too, by taking me away a bit from the pressure of the weekend.

Everything went well on the Friday, but on the Saturday morning the heavens opened and Superpole was very nearly disastrous.

I had a crash at turn three on my first flying lap and hyper-extended my left shoulder, which I had hurt before. Luckily, I was able to get back to the garage and get my head together while the crew fixed the damage to the bike. I went out again and took pole position with a gap of over a second to the second-fastest guy. But my shoulder was pretty painful and it could have been a big problem. I was fortunate though, because, on Fab's recommendation, French physio Philippe Petite had been travelling with me all season. He strapped me quite heavily for race one that afternoon, which was still wet but threatening to dry out. When the lights went out, I took the holeshot and set off at a really comfortable pace. I grabbed the race by the scruff of the neck and just found myself pulling away from everyone.

I'd been in a wet race with a big lead at Magny-Cours back in my Honda days, and crashed out at the first chicane. That was going through my head, but then I thought if I started slowing down and thinking about the championship, that's when I was going to make a mistake.

So I just kept my pace and, even when I started short-shifting and rolling off the gas a bit in the last few laps, I was still pulling away from everyone and crossed the line with a big stand-up wheelie and a gap of more than 16 seconds to Marco Melandri in second place.

That feeling more than made up for the two previous championships when I didn't win a race to secure the title. Standing on the top step in the middle of the podium as world champion felt incredible.

It was made even more special when my mum and dad, Richard, Tatia, Jake, Tyler and Kev all joined me there to celebrate the third championship. To have all the people who were closest to me up there on the podium together was something I will never, ever forget.

We had a celebratory dinner in hospitality on that Saturday night and nobody got to bed too late because there was another race to be done on the Sunday. I knew there wasn't to be any kind of celebration the next night either, because the team were all desperate to get back to Barcelona to vote in the referendum for Catalonian independence from Spain.

I woke up on that Sunday morning feeling like a world champion and got into race two with another significant target to aim for.

During our dominant year in 2015, I'd come within four points of the Superbike season points record set by Colin Edwards when he won the championship in 2002. With our incredible season in 2017, it looked like it was game on but, after I crashed out at Donington Park when the rear tyre exploded, it was going to be tight. It got a whole lot tighter when in that second race at Magny-Cours, Eugene Laverty crashed in front of me just before the final chicane. His bike slid towards me and hit my foot so hard that it broke the footpeg off my bike, so I couldn't continue and got a DNF.

The last two rounds were at circuits where I had never won. To break the record, I was now going to have to win all four races. No pressure.

CHAPTER 16

HOMECOMING

EUGENE LAVERTY'S CRASH that took me out of race two at Magny-Cours brought me back down to earth with a big bump, but it didn't take away from that incredible weekend and my third successive World Superbike Championship. You hear a lot of world champions say the best feeling is winning their first, but, for me, it's definitely that third one – it was off the scale. I look back on that and think, how could I ever achieve that consistency and win rate again? It was almost trippy how mind-blowing it was.

What wasn't so trippy was getting stopped for speeding on the way to the airstrip where the jet was waiting to take us home, about an hour from Magny-Cours. We had a pre-booked landing slot at Belfast City Airport and, if we missed that, it was going to cost a lot of money and foul up the evening. So maybe the €130 on-the-spot fine from the gendarme was worth it. We made the flight and Joanne texted me when we were onboard saying there were a lot of people gathering in Belfast at the airport.

That didn't really prepare me for what we saw there, though: what we landed into blew my mind even more.

There were loads of people I'd never met, kids and parents and grandparents, all wishing me well. It was also so nice to see others, like Jeremy McWilliams, who had been so influential in the early part of my career and a great sounding board over the years.

I was also amazed to see Brian Reid at the airport. Brian is a road racing hero in Northern Ireland and was Formula TT world champion twice in the mid-1980s. He also won five TTs. In 2015, during the slow-down lap of my first championship win at Jerez, I'd stopped a couple of times to put on two replica helmets. One was Joey Dunlop's and the other was Brian Reid's – two riders who did so much to put Northern Ireland on the world motorcycle racing map.

It was an epic homecoming, and for the rest of that amazing week, the BBC Northern Ireland TV crew that had been with us all weekend in Magny-Cours stayed with us. They were in the Culloden Hotel in Belfast where the Northern Ireland football squad was staying ahead of a vital World Cup qualifying game against Germany later in the week. I was really touched when Michael O'Neill, the manager, and a few of the players came down to congratulate me.

But the evening was mostly about saying hello and thanks to members of my family and close friends who had supported me so much through my career. At that point, we had to turn off the cameras because it got pretty emotional!

There was a tour of TV and radio studios for a load of interviews and then a visit to my home town of Ballyclare. That was such a humbling experience, kick-started by a massive posse of motorcyclists who followed our car down to the Sixmile Leisure Centre. The place was absolutely packed, and I was told people had been queuing for hours in the chilly autumn weather to get in. Some people weren't even able to get through the doors but waited patiently outside to get a selfie or an autograph afterwards. It was the most incredible, emotional night and really underlined for me that, even though I'd lived on the Isle of Man for nine years, this place was my home and these were my people.

To cap the week off, Tatia and I went to Northern Ireland's World Cup qualifier against Germany at Windsor Park. In one of the most important games in the history of football in Northern Ireland, they brought me out onto the field, the crowd was singing, the atmosphere was incredible, and moments like that just stick with you forever. I was in a bubble and on cloud nine at the same time.

THAT WEEK THOUGH, somewhere deep in the back of my mind, there was the thought about winning the races in Jerez and Qatar to round off the season.

The following weekend was the Monster Energy Cup in Las Vegas, an end-of-season Supercross race that had been on my bucket list for a while. Monster have become one of my biggest personal sponsors, so I reached out to them to hook up me and my two mechanics, Uri and Arturo, for the event. We had a fabulous weekend in Las Vegas, although jet-lag didn't have any respect for our two-night stay. Unfortunately, we went a bit too hard on the first night and when we got to the official Monster party in the Cromwell Hotel on the second night, we lasted all of about 10 minutes. After our first drink we were all like zombies, saying, 'We should probably go to bed!' The Supercross had been amazing though, and both Monster and Kawasaki had looked after us like kings. During the opening ceremonies, they brought me onto the track and interviewed me live on Fox Sports, and we got to stand above the start line in the huge Monster hospitality.

The hangover and jet-lag had cleared by the time we rocked up at Jerez a couple of weeks later. I had this plan to try to put winning the championship, and all that had happened since, behind us and focus on that points record. Jerez had been a bogey track for me. After those two fourth places in my first championship year, we had gone 3–2 in 2016 and I'd never even had a sniff of winning there. I needed to get my mind back on winning and working out what we had to do to achieve that.

With about four laps to go in race one, I was running in second but closing down on Marco Melandri. Then he had a technical problem and had to retire, so finally I got that win, albeit with a little help from a broken Ducati.

One down, three to go.

Starting race two from ninth on the grid, I managed to get to the front on about lap two or three and was able to control the race from there, eventually winning by about three seconds.

Suddenly, we were heading to the final round at Qatar with the record wide open. It was all I could think about.

Circuits have become so much more than strips of tarmac and corners to me. For the last few years, especially since the kids were born, Qatar has been a great place to combine the last round of the season with a few days of early winter sun. What's more, because we practise and race at night there, it's a great chance to spend some time kicking back at the Ritz-Carlton hotel pool during the day to enjoy a relaxing build-up to the race.

Since I had secured the championship at Magny-Cours, the organisers had announced some new technical regulations they were planning to introduce for the 2018 season. They were proposing to restrict rpm levels in the bikes' engines and use other 'balancing tools' in an attempt to even out the different manufacturers' performances. In other words, it was 'Stop Kawasaki'! We were the victims of our own success and, like the reverse grid system that they introduced for 2017, they wanted to make the racing closer. It's something F1 and MotoGP have been trying to do for years, and there was no reason World Superbikes should be any different.

I had been talking about this with Pere and Kawasaki and I'd told them I would like to finish the season racing a bike that was similar to the one I would be riding in 2018. It meant riding with the reduced rpm level, even though Kawasaki hadn't yet developed the engine specifically to run at the lower rev limit. I had been suggesting this idea to give us a head start on the regulations, but there was also a worry that it might prevent me from achieving that target of Colin Edwards's points record.

So we went into FP1 at Qatar on the 2017 specification bike, but for FP2 we adjusted the engine to restrict it to the proposed rev limits we'd be running the following season – basically more than 1000rpm lower.

But I was still fast. So we stuck with it for the rest of practice and qualifying and the races. I was riding with so much confidence that year, so much belief in what I could do on the bike. Nobody knew what we'd done, unless they were clever and were watching us all weekend and noticing that we were suddenly going through the speed trap in the bottom three instead of the top three.

It turned into an incredibly special weekend and, even with that confidence in me and the bike, I amazed myself and won both races, beating the points record. I'd scored 556 points and had a third successive world title in the bag. We'd had such an incredible season, winning 16 out of 26 races and finishing second in seven others.

Surely it was time to relax and go on holiday? No, 2017 wasn't quite done with me yet.

Earlier in the season, during the Misano weekend, I'd been up early one morning and had gone for breakfast in the team's hospitality unit. I'm a bit spoilt really and the chefs there make me whatever I fancy for breakfast. When I walked in for my eggs and toast, Kev started bowing at me, taking the piss, and Guim, who was sitting there having a coffee, started giving me a round of applause and calling me Sir Jonathan. I said, 'OK, what the hell's going on?' and Kev replied, 'Haven't you checked your phone this morning? You've just been awarded an MBE in the Queen's birthday honours list!'

I had to pick my jaw up from off the floor.

I'd received a letter weeks before which asked something like, would I object to receiving some kind of award. In a world of my own, I guess I just ticked the 'no' box and sent it back and didn't really think any more about it. But here I was in Italy reading on my phone that I was to be a Member of the Most Excellent Order of the British Empire, which, in the UK, is a way of recognising someone's achievements in a particular field – it might be work for a charity, in public service or entertainment, sport or, in my case, for services to motorcycling.

My appointment at Buckingham Palace came in the middle of the five-day end-of-season test at Jerez. Even though an MBE meant nothing to my Spanish team, they gave me the day off to fly back to London.

I was more nervous in the waiting room than I've ever been on any grid. I was one of the later recipients, and while I was waiting I watched the others pick up their awards on the big screens all around the room. I was thinking about what I might say to Prince William when he gave me the medal. I knew he liked bikes but wasn't sure if he followed racing. Well, if he didn't he'd certainly read up on his briefing notes pretty well – I checked for an earpiece to see if he was getting any prompts, but I couldn't see anything. He started by congratulating me on my three titles. I replied by saying thanks and added, 'I hear you're pretty into your bikes as well.' That worked OK because he opened up and talked about himself for a bit while I recovered my nerves. Then it was goodbye and the handshake and exit plan that we'd been briefed on, and then a chance for some photos in the back room with Tatia and my parents, who had come over for the ceremony.

It was an amazing experience, the start of many in the off-season. My only regret is that I was so busy during it that I never really stopped to take in all these things that were happening.

The weekend after the season finale in Qatar, I rented a huge villa in Marbella for me and my team to go and party, and we had a pretty massive weekend. That was followed by visiting all the motorcycle trade fairs like EICMA in Milan and Motorcycle Live in Birmingham. Then there was another special ceremony at the annual FIM awards when medals are handed out by the world's governing body for motor-cycle sport – the Fédération Internationale de Motocyclisme. This is a truly memorable occasion, because basically you have to be a world champion to get invited. It's the first time it really sinks in that you are a champion and you get the real FIM medal to prove it. In 2017 it was held in Andorra and Tatia and I had a great evening, but as soon as that was finished I was off on another PR trail. After three hours' sleep, there was an 04.00 call for a lift to Barcelona to get on a plane to Japan and Thailand.

There was one final experience waiting for me when I got home: the BBC's Sports Personality of the Year. I had been asking Stephen and Gary when the BBC Northern Ireland documentary might come out and they kept telling me that they wouldn't know until the SPOTY shortlist was published.

It's a pretty big deal in the UK, in which 12 leading athletes from a wide range of different sports are nominated for a public vote around a massive live TV show that reviews the year in sport. I was super-happy just to get nominated but also nervous about the response. Would the public vote for me? Would they even know who I was? There are only 12 nominees and, while I knew I had no chance of winning, I didn't want to come bottom in a public vote either!

The event itself fell in that crazy busy period and I never really got the chance to stop, take it all in and enjoy it. But Tatia had been managing a lot on her own with the kids while I'd been away fulfilling PR duties, so at the very least I wanted this to be a big night out for her. A couple of days before, we went to Liverpool, which was hosting the ceremony, with my mum, Chloe, Richard and his girlfriend Leanne, and on the day of the awards the girls had a bit of a pamper while Richard and I took the boys to a trampoline park.

The night before the show, I went into Liverpool's Echo Arena for a rehearsal because they wanted me to ride a bike on to the stage. The producers were looking for a lot of engine revving and noise, but it was nerve-wracking enough for me. They wanted me to ride up a ramp which had a really tight turn at the end of the aisle. I wanted to play it cool and ride onto it without dabbing my feet down, but I never managed it in rehearsals. I also nearly dropped the bike on the stage! I'm so used to riding up to one of my mechanics in the pit-lane and them taking the bike from me that I forgot this road bike had a sidestand. It very nearly went over the first time I tried to climb off it! I calmed my nerves later with a couple of beers in The Cavern – I love Liverpool and I've spent a lot of time there. It's such a vibrant city.

On the big night, we had to go and do the red carpet with live TV, which was a new experience, stopping for a quick word with the various media that were lined up. I obviously wasn't the most well known of all the people arriving, but the BBC provided us with a researcher to do the introductions, sparing us any awkward moments. The journalists were pretty well prepared with information about the nominees, but they seemed genuinely excited by motorcycle racing and my story, because it's still relatively low profile.

In a big function room before the show, I met up with a few familiar faces: there was Foggy, John McGuinness, Ian Hutchinson and James Toseland, who were all there as guests, and they were all super-happy that bike racing was in the spotlight once again. It was good to calm the nerves by having a beer with them. We went into the arena for the event itself and took our seats in the front row, but halfway through the show they asked us to swap places with the ice skaters Jayne Torvill and Christopher Dean. A camera was coming down and they wanted a clear shot of them, but as soon as the camera was gone, they told us to swap back again. That's live TV!

I'd been reading on a few of the betting websites that I was something like the fifth favourite, which I was pretty happy with. My worst nightmare was to be the guy coming last, the one that nobody picked up the phone to vote for. So I was just enjoying a glitzy date night with my wife with absolutely no expectations of any prizes. I couldn't face voting for myself – it just felt a bit weird – but Tatia was sitting beside me ringing the number over and over. After a few times, I just had to ask her to stop embarrassing me!

The lines closed and they announced that third place was going to Jonnie Peacock, an amazing Paralympic sprinter, and after that I thought that was me done. If I was ever going to be placed, then maybe I could have just squeezed a third. I had a big sigh of relief and thought at least I'd had a couple of drinks on the BBC. But then Kenny Dalglish read my name out as the runner-up!

I honestly could not believe it.

I was on a list of 12 nominees alongside people like Lewis Hamilton, Chris Froome, and others. To even be on that list was incredible, but to be put ahead of most of them by the public was, well … just mind-blowing. I stumbled up to the stage in a bit of a daze, desperately trying not to fall over. I guess I was kind of straight-faced, but it was just surreal.

One of the best moments of the night came after I had collected my award and I was off to the side with Jonnie Peacock, waiting for them to announce the winner. Anthony Joshua had been leading in the polls and was favourite with the bookies, so I was looking directly at him to see his reaction when they announced his name. But then they announced the winner was Mo Farah.

It was really cool seeing Anthony's face, because he seemed so genuinely happy for Mo and was clapping so enthusiastically. He'd just won the world heavyweight boxing title and everyone was expecting him to win SPOTY. I thought what an amazing guy to be so generous in his support for the winner.

We had a little press conference afterwards and a few interviews, so it was probably 45 minutes before I got to the after-party, where I hooked up with Tatia and my family who were busy getting a selfie with Rebecca Ferguson. The finger buffet had gone by then, so I got a few beers in and had a great chat with Charlie Stayt, the *BBC Breakfast* presenter, who was really interested in bike racing, even though he thought we were all mad. We all danced to the most incredible band and it was certainly an after-party that lived up to the occasion.

The morning after, as we waited for take-off on the Melbourne-bound plane for another winter in Australia, I thought about the whirlwind that had happened after winning that third title at Magny-Cours: the welcome in Belfast, the Supercross in the USA, the last two rounds and the Superbike points record, the party in Marbella, the MBE ceremony at Buckingham Palace, the BBC Sports Personality of the Year awards.

But I was particularly drawn back to the PR trip to Japan and Thailand, which I'd rushed off to having had no sleep after the FIM awards ceremony.

The hospitality in Japan is always incredible and this time they picked me up from Osaka airport in a helicopter and flew me to the Kawasaki Heavy Industries factory at Akashi. There were hundreds and hundreds of staff out to welcome me, to clap and wave banners. I realised just how much the wins and championships mean to those guys, thousands of miles away from the racing. It was amazingly surreal and really humbling.

My two days in Japan were strictly scheduled, almost down to the second, but we ate in the best restaurants and stayed in the finest hotels. They treated me like a king and I remember sitting back in my hotel room in a rare spare moment one afternoon and reflecting on it all.

I thought about all the tough times me and my family had been through during the 25 years I've been doing this. The sacrifices I have made and, more importantly, the sacrifices those I love have had to make. The injuries and rehab that require nursing and support, not just from professionals but from family, too. The moments of self-doubt or frustration that require confidence-building and reassurance. The dilemmas relating to the next career move that require clarity, knowledge and experience. The negativity and criticism you inevitably encounter on social media that need to be countered with optimism and positivity.

Those closest to us provide so much.

They sacrifice the most without having the opportunity to enjoy the massive rewards that can balance it all out. They get no appreciation from the public, they spray no podium champagne and they take no applause at the award ceremonies.

It is, I think, one of the most genuine expressions of unconditional love.

As I sat in that hotel room in Japan at the end of 2017, I didn't feel special, or important, or talented, or successful, or clever. I just felt so incredibly fortunate and blessed to live this life.

Chapter 17

FOUR OF A KIND

FOUR OF A KIND

IT TOOK A while for the dust to settle on 2017, particularly after a really tough year in 2016, when winning the championship felt more like a relief than a triumph in itself. I'd won almost twice as many races, broken the record for the most number of points in a season, won my third championship, finished runner-up in the BBC Sports Personality of the Year and been awarded the MBE. It felt like I was at the absolute peak of my career, that I couldn't possibly go any higher. What was 2018 going to bring? Far too much to cover in one chapter, that's for sure.

Despite all the amazing highs of 2017, it wasn't long before I started worrying about whether my career had reached a plateau and that the only possible way was down. I wasn't so concerned about whether I could continue performing well on the bike; it was more that one day another rider would be faster or another bike would be better. It wasn't even really the fear of losing or letting anyone down that troubled me – it just started to dawn on me that inevitably, my time at the top was limited. I loved being inside my winning bubble, with my family and my team, and I wasn't looking forward to it being popped. I don't know whether it's my philosophy, my personality, my faith or just my general attitude towards life, but I've always felt that no-one can really have it that good for very long. It can't all be sunshine and rainbows. Sooner or later, life will come along and hand you a shit sandwich.

The first sign that things might not run as smoothly for me in 2018 came when I went to my annual motocross training camp in January and had a crash. It was a silly little off but somehow I managed to completely slice open the ring finger on my right hand – the same finger that I had damaged badly in my World Supersport debut in Qatar ten years previously. It just opened up like a sausage, so I had to have immediate surgery and, desperate for it to heal as quickly as possible, I was frantically hunting for oxygen chambers in Spain that might help speed up the process. Just one month later, I had a massive crash at turn 11 on the first day of the pre-race test in Australia ahead of the opening round. I was pretty badly shaken up and couldn't help but think about that ominous shit sandwich. In a panic, I insisted that we completely turned the bike around and in doing so, we managed to destroy the great base setting that we'd developed during the winter. As if that wasn't bad enough, I managed to pick up some sort of virus on the Wednesday before the race. So I went into the weekend with zero energy, a bad finger and new technical regulations limiting the revs on a bike that I wasn't certain was going to work for me.

Pere came to me before the first race and said, 'Listen, the situation is not ideal, you're not feeling well, so just go out and do the best you can.' I ended up having some serious tyre issues in the first race and was lucky to cross the line in fifth place – my worst result on the Kawasaki and the first time I hadn't led the championships since the beginning of 2015. Obviously this didn't help my anxiety about the season ahead.

However, after that race it was clear that a lot of other riders had suffered the same tyre blistering as I had and Pirelli felt it was unsafe for the tyres to go the full distance in race two. So, the organisers introduced a mandatory tyre change at half distance, on either lap 10 or 11. The next day, I was feeling a little better physically and more confident that the tyres would hold together. I was also encouraged by some changes we'd made to the bike, so I was able to give a much better account of myself and finished just behind Melandri after a sprint to the line on the final lap. It was still a horrible weekend but at least I'd salvaged a podium.

We stayed in Australia until the next round in Thailand and I had a lot to think about. I was third in the championship, with even my team-mate Tom in front of me after two races at a circuit where he's never performed that strongly. But I got myself healthy, rode some motocross, recovered and prepared well, so that by the time we arrived in Buriram I was in a more positive frame of mind. Thankfully, this paid off and we got back on track with pole position and a race one win. It felt so good and such a relief to be back on the top step, although the feeling was short-lived because I had a few issues with the brakes in the second race. Starting from the third row was hard enough and the problems led to a few uncharacteristic mistakes from me, which meant I could finish no higher than fourth. We had definitely made progress, but being off the podium again at a track where we'd previously performed really well, especially after the pace we showed in race one, was tough. However, I was determined to stay focused and positive. It would have been so easy to say 'Well, I've had my moment; this is kind of what I expected.' But, with help from family and team, I had managed to stay upbeat and single-minded. I was also hopeful and felt that we were moving forward.

We headed back to Europe and to Aragon, which had been a happy hunting ground for Chaz Davies, and we knew we still had a lot of work to do. Happily, I won the first race and was second to Chaz in the second. Going 1–2 was thrilling and I was just so relieved that things were finally starting to pick up – something that continued in the following round in Assen, which has always been my own happy hunting ground. I felt confident heading into that weekend and won race one. I was feeling good about race two as well, but Tom's no stranger to Assen and his strategy from pole position was clear: put his head down and build a big lead as early as possible. He did the job and rode one of his best races of the season, while I came from ninth on the grid to finish second.

We went straight from Assen to test at Brno in the Czech Republic which was back on the calendar after six years without hosting a race. On the last day of the test, Pere came with a plan that he had been developing having worked with Kawasaki for the upcoming Suzuka 8 Hours race, where the bikes use different tyres and run with a slightly different chassis set-up. He had been working on a few ideas that he wanted me to test on our version.

Our main focus was adjusting the weight distribution by altering the distance between the front and rear axles. The changes made the bike so much more stable: I felt like I was riding on rails, the difference was incredible. Pere and the team clearly shared my determination – they had kept pushing through the rocky start to 2018 and worked on changes to the bike that would really transform things for us. It felt as if we were emerging from the tunnel into bright sunlight, and when we went to Imola a couple of weeks later, our optimism and hard work were rewarded. Taking pole position and doubling up there felt particularly special because Imola is Ducati's home track. To do it in style in front of all their factory staff and passionate fans was the biggest confidence boost for us because we'd so often been on the back foot there behind Chaz and his Ducati.

The team gave me an incredible bike again at Donington Park in the UK but once again, 2018 wasn't proving to be a straightforward season. I finished on the podium in both races but felt that I let the guys down a bit because I had huge arm-pump issues. It didn't help that Michael van der Mark was on fire, riding unbelievably well to take his first two World Superbike wins. Despite this, I tried to remain confident as we headed back to Brno where thankfully, we took an amazingly satisfying victory in race one – the record-breaking 60th win you read about earlier in the book.

Race two was a completely different story, though. I got an OK start from the third row of the grid and by lap three,

I was battling with Tom for fifth as we headed into the first uphill chicane at turn 11. I ran in really fast to try to pass Tom but deliberately left enough space for him in case he was going to try to cut back. As we went through the right-hander at turn 12, instead of cutting back underneath me he picked his bike up and rode straight to the edge of the track, running across the front of my bike, taking me down and leaving me fuming in the gravel trap.

Even though I still had a good hold on the championship, I lost a lot of points that day. Thankfully, at the following round at Laguna Seca in California, the races pretty much looked after themselves. We took the double – testament to the great shape of the bike – and heading into Misano for the last round before the summer break we were all on a high. Things even began to feel like the unstoppable year before. Our results in Italy were fantastic and we made it another double, but Michael van der Mark was in great form again and in race two, especially, I had to give everything and empty the tank to beat him. The weekend was another massive boost for the championship but some bad news after my race one win on the Saturday put things sharply into perspective.

William Dunlop, part of the legendary Northern Irish road racing dynasty, son of Robert, brother of Michael and nephew of Joey, had died after crashing at the Skerries races near Dublin. Apart from being a lovely bloke, he was a very successful racer, winning at the North West 200 and the Ulster Grand Prix, and finishing on the podium several times at the Isle of Man TT. I couldn't imagine what his family was going through, particularly as they'd already lost both Joey and Robert to crashes. William's partner Janine was pregnant with their second daughter at the time and it was a truly horrible reminder of the dangers involved in our sport. But thoughts of William powered me through the final laps of race two at Misano and I dedicated that victory to him on the podium.

I didn't get much of a summer break because Pere, Uri and I travelled to Japan to test for the Suzuka 8 Hours race – something I'd agreed to do at the end of 2017 when I was looking for a fresh challenge. I'd won it with Honda in 2012 and although I hadn't been back there since, I was pretty fast and felt comfortable from the off. I love Suzuka and the test went well, so it really whetted my appetite for the whole event, especially because Kawasaki hadn't won the race for such a long time.

Even though I was going as World Superbike champion, we were the real underdogs because motorcycles are not even Kawasaki's main business. They're more famous in Japan for manufacturing trains, ships, helicopters and heavy industrial equipment. They also make the engines for Boeing's 787 jetliner. Looking at the big support infrastructure behind Honda, Yoshimura Suzuki and Yamaha, I felt even more determined to secure the victory for the little bike factory from Akashi.

Having set a great lap time in practice, we were in pole position for the race. My team-mate Leon Haslam started well enough in the wet but the rain passed through quite quickly and he made an early pit-stop, which allowed me to put my head down and get us into the lead. The first half of the race turned into a ding-dong Superbike fight between me and Leon on the Kawasaki and Lowes and van der Mark on the Yamaha. However, at the end of the fourth hour and my second stint, the bike started running out of fuel on the back straight, which made it difficult to get back to the pits. It was a massive fuel miscalculation and set off a series of events that shouldn't have happened. Leon went back out and held his own but then the rain came down during my third stint and the organisers sent out safety cars. Because of the time we'd lost, I got stuck behind the second safety car instead of the first one, which was ahead of the race leader, so we lost another half a lap. To make matters worse, I crashed behind the pace car at 60kmh. It was a freak crash and something I'm still embarrassed about, and it ruined any chance of victory that we had. We eventually finished third while Yamaha won for the fourth consecutive year. Unsurprisingly, Lowes and van der Mark were very chipper on the podium, so I resolved to turn the page on Suzuka and get back to my team and my territory in Europe.

Returning to the championship seemed to mark a turning point in the season when I could finally put my anxiety behind me. After the race two incident at Brno, we were undefeated for the rest of the year. It was great to get back to a double win at Portimao in Portugal, the venue for my World Superbike debut, before returning to Magny-Cours where I'd won the previous year's championship – this brought back some really special memories. It was game on to get it done in the first race because I knew that if I won

and Chaz finished lower than second, the fourth championship was mine. I got my head down from lap one and I
checked out with a great stand-up wheelie at the end, just
like the year before. I couldn't believe we'd done it again.

In the days leading up to Magny-Cours, Biel, the team's
marketing manager, talked to me about an idea he'd had for
a celebration if we won the fourth title that weekend – something along the lines of 'Four of a Kind'. Getting some real
people dressed up in my leathers and helmets from the previous championship years felt fitting, so Biel got on with
making up some cards while I sourced some of my old gear.
It was great to have Fab, Uri, my chief mechanic, and Eva,
the team's press officer, dressed up to look like me as I
stopped during the slow-down lap. I walked really slowly
over to this card table where these other versions of me were
waiting and picked up a hand of four over-sized aces. But
the best part of winning the championship again with
another race victory was getting back to parc fermé and
celebrating with the rest of the team and my family. Seeing
the happiness on the faces of the people closest to you makes
every win incredibly special. To see their faces after winning
a fourth championship was on another level.

Normally, the winning team sends a senior representative
to the podium to collect the manufacturers' award from the
organisers. Guim, the team manager, always nominates
someone from Kawasaki or a sponsor to pick up the award;
he's never been up there himself. He was running out of
people to nominate and everyone felt that surely, it was his
turn, but he asked my dad if he'd like to go. Unsurprisingly,

Dad's response was, 'Oh, I'm not sure. I'll be too nervous,' but Guim had already told the organisers, who'd prepared a graphic with his name for the TV. It really was the cherry on top for me: to win my fourth championship and to have standing next to me on the podium the guy who started it all off in a little garden in Kilwaughter.

For race two the following day, I rode with a special commemorative helmet and fairing to celebrate the championship, and having fully rid myself of my anxieties about the season, I wasn't too worried about jinxing the result. Taking my 14th win of 2018 was the perfect way to end another wonderful weekend and, with the team packed up and gone, I went to bed reasonably early that night and reflected on the fourth title. It meant so much more than breaking Carl Fogarty's race win record earlier in the season because championships are the first stat that you look at on a rider's CV. I felt so proud of what I'd achieved. I finally felt comfortable being talked about in the same terms as Foggy.

The fourth championship wasn't the only record that I had a chance of breaking that year. By the time we got to Qatar, I had the opportunity to match Doug Polen's 1991 record for the highest number of season wins. But despite having tucked the front at turn two in my second lap of the practice session, I went on to win the first race and while I was glowing with pride about that achievement, I was also relishing the chance to set a new record in race two.

Sadly, it wasn't to be, as there was a massive desert storm on the Sunday. Wind and rain destroyed some of the paddock show and podium constructions, and the track was in a really bad state, which disrupted the schedule and put race two in serious doubt. All the riders wanted to go ahead for the grand finale, but it was eventually agreed that it should be cancelled. The championship positions had already been decided and the conditions were just too dangerous.

It was a massive anticlimax and at the time I was disappointed with how the season ended. But after a couple more days by the pool and having had the chance to unwind a bit, it began to sink in that 2018 had truly been another amazing season, especially given how badly it had started.

Beating Foggy's win record, going undefeated for the final 11 races and matching Doug Polen's record were big enough achievements in themselves, but I was especially proud that we hadn't faltered when things were tough at the beginning, when I was feeling particularly anxious about how the season would pan out.

More than anything, 2018 taught me that I can afford to be a lot more rational and analytical if the results don't come. The season began with quite a bit of stress, anxiety and a load of new challenges but, with help from my team and my family, we toughed it out. To top off the year, we spent Christmas as a family in Northern Ireland in an incredible new home that we had moved into in August.

Motivation is the one thing I've never had any trouble finding. Looking ahead to 2019, we have a good team, a strong Kawasaki package and the knowledge that we can be consistent over the course of a 13-round championship. I know my own strengths and weaknesses and, of course, my rivals' as well. I'm never the kind of person to get complacent and although I still worry about injuries and obstacles that are out of my control, I'm not burdened by the same anxieties or concerns that I felt after winning the third championship. A few bad results or a dip in confidence are things that I've learned how to ride through – I finally feel equipped to cope with anything that comes my way, be it the bad or the good. Bring on 2019.

ACKNOWLEDGEMENTS

WHILE I HAVE been so fortunate to achieve the dream I set out for myself after many, many years, it would never have become a reality if a whole bunch of people hadn't believed in me. Right now, I feel that I'm a long way from waking up from the dream, but I know that someday I'm going to have to. Nothing this good could possibly last forever.

Not surprisingly, the most important people in my life have played their part in making the dream real, particularly over the past three or four years – my wife Tatia and our two boys, Jake and Tyler. They are my rock, my reference point and my refuge whenever things get too much – good or bad.

My own family – Mum, Dad, Richard, Kristofer and Chloe – provided the love, the support and the solid foundation on which the dream was built, from the minute I first threw my leg over that little Italjet. They've been with me every step of the way, every turn of every wheel, and they're still there providing the encouragement for me to keep doing what I do, the consolation when it doesn't go to plan and the congratulations when it does.

303

Tatia's family in Cowes, Phillip Island – John and Barb Weston, her brother Jarv and his wife Kara, together with family friend Kaye – have given me and my sons another home and another family on the other side of the world. Our life there is a paradise, far away from a northern hemisphere winter, that allows me to throw off the hangover of one season and prepare in the most stress-free and incredibly relaxed way possible for the next.

There are so many others who have helped to make my dream come true, and although it would be impossible to list each individual here, every single one of them knows what they've done to help me along this journey and how much I value and appreciate their time and support. Some of them are here, but, especially to those who I may have inadvertently left off this list, you have all played an incredibly important part in making it all happen and I will always be so, so grateful to you.

Andrew Pitt

From being a team-mate to becoming one of my best mates. Whether you realise it or not, you taught me so much and you've been a great friend to me since I've started, and I love the Team Pitt–Rea holidays we have with all the gang.

Arai Helmets

Thanks to Wendy Hearn for bringing me into the family when I started road racing, and to Ingmar, Marcel and Pierre for supporting me through all my World Championship career.

ACKNOWLEDGEMENTS

BBC Northern Ireland

Stephen and Gary, thanks for all you have done for me in helping to build my profile, even when I was riding around chasing the MX dream. So proud of the 'Three in a row' documentary.

Chris Pike

You taught me so much and helped me understand how to extract the best out of myself and the bike during some challenging years.

Chuck Aksland

Thanks for always getting the deal done. I've enjoyed working with you from 2009 and the friendship we have, even if I have to break your balls from time to time.

Gabriele Mazzarolo

To the man behind Alpinestars, thanks for bringing me into the Astars family at such a young age and for keeping me safe and looking cool.

Gary Price

What can I say, Gaz? Thanks for being there, mate, it's been amazing sharing a lot of this journey with you from the beginning.

Gary Ross
Together with Todd and Kathy and everyone at International Racers, you have taken care of the business end of my life and made sure that my family is always safe and secure.

Gavin Hunt
Gav, you bloody legend. Thanks for being a great mate and never sugar-coating things if I ride shit. Can't wait for the next MX trip!

Keith Amor
Dude, half the stories won't make it past this book's legal team, but what a time we had together, and you put the laughs in the tough times. I'll never forget Nürburgring 2013 when you put your life on hold to look after me. Legend!

Kevin Havenhand
Mate, words will never thank you enough for living this dream with us. You are our rock and we couldn't do this without you.

Guim Roda
You have taught me more about myself and how to manage my inner chimp than racing itself. You never switch off, and this is why we keep getting stronger.

Joanne McNeill

Joanne, thanks for everything you do for us, and getting us in a position to put my life on paper. Looking forward to what the future holds.

Linda Pelham

Thanks for believing in me and giving me the opportunity to realise my dreams. If it wasn't for you, I would not be World Champion.

Monster Energy

Being part of the Monster family is amazing. Thanks Mitch and Tommy for all your support over these last three seasons.

Pere Riba

You built the whole Team65 winning machine together with Uri, Arturo, Javier, Pau and Fabien. Thanks for making it so much fun.

Ronald ten Kate

When things got tough, you guys never gave up. I love that about you all. What we did together in 2014 was amazing.

Robert Watherston

The one guy inside Honda that had the balls to put effort into the Superbike programme. After you joined SBK, every-one had a reason for optimism.

Stephen Booth

Boothy, what a guy! Not many get me like you do, mate. I've loved doing this book with you, just have to apologise for stretching deadlines. But trying to win a fourth Championship is a good enough reason to be late.

Steve Guttridge

I'm convinced you hired me because I'm a motocross guy at heart. Such a cool boss, and I love working with you.

Career Statistics

Personal

Height: 176cm

Weight: 70kg

First bike: Italjet 50

Sponsors: Alpinestars, Arai Helmets, Monster Energy, Oakley, Carole Nash, Pata Snacks

Race Number: 1

2019 team: Kawasaki Racing Team

2019 bike: Kawasaki ZX-10RR

Career Highlights

Four-time World Superbike Champion (2015–18)

Most points in a single WSBK season (556 in 2017)

Highest number of WSBK race wins (71 to end of 2018 season)

Joint-highest number of wins (17) in a single WSBK season (2018)

First British winner Suzuka 8 Hours (2012)

British Supersport Championship – 1 season

British Superbike Championship – 3 seasons

World Supersport Championship – 1 season

World Superbike Championship – 10 seasons

Awarded MBE in 2017 Queen's Birthday Honours

BBC Sports Personality of the Year 2017 – runner-up

Career By Year

2018 WSBK

	Poles	Races	Podiums	Wins	Fastest Laps	Final Pos
Kawasaki	2	25	22	17	14	CHAMPION

	AUS	THA	SPA	NED	ITA	GBR	CZE	USA	ITA	POR	FRA	ARG	QAT
Race 1	5	1	1	1	1	2	1	1	1	1	1	1	1
Race 2	2	4	2	2	1	3	DNF	1	1	1	1	1	C

2017 WSBK

	Poles	Races	Podiums	Wins	Fastest Laps	Final Pos
Kawasaki	6	26	24	16	14	CHAMPION

	AUS	THA	SPA	NED	ITA	GBR	ITA	USA	GER	POR	FRA	SPA	QAT
Race 1	1	1	1	1	2	19	3	2	2	1	1	1	1
Race 2	1	1	2	1	2	1	2	1	2	1	21	1	1

2016 WSBK

	Poles	Races	Podiums	Wins	Fastest Laps	Final Pos
Kawasaki	2	26	23	9	6	CHAMPION

	AUS	THA	SPA	NED	ITA	MAL	GBR	ITA	USA	GER	FRA	SPA	QAT
Race 1	1	1	2	1	2	2	3	1	1	23	4	3	2
Race 2	1	2	3	1	2	3	2	1	18	1	2	2	3

2015 WSBK

	Poles	Races	Podiums	Wins	Fastest Laps	Final Pos
Kawasaki	2	26	23	14	11	CHAMPION

	AUS	THA	SPA	NED	IMO	GBR	POR	ITA	USA	MAL	SPA	FRA	QAT
Race 1	1	1	1	1	1	2	1	2	3	1	4	1	2
Race 2	2	1	2	1	1	2	1	1	3	2	4	1	18

2014 WSBK

	Poles	Races	Podiums	Wins	Fastest Laps	Final Pos
Honda	1	24	9	4	2	THIRD

	AUS	SPA	NED	IMO	GBR	MAL	ITA	POR	USA	SPA	FRA	QAT
Race 1	6	3	3	1	6	6	7	5	6	4	3	4
Race 2	5	5	1	1	6	6	5	1	3	5	R	2

2013 WSBK

	Poles	Races	Podiums	Wins	Fastest Laps	Final Pos
Honda	0	18	4	1	1	NINTH

	AUS	SPA	NED	ITA	GBR	POR	IMO	RUS	GBR	GER
Race 1	8	4	2	8	4	R	R	4	1	R
Race 2	8	15	4	R	11	3	2	-	4	-

2012 WSBK

	Poles	Races	Podiums	Wins	Fastest Laps	Final Pos
Honda	0	27	6	2	0	FIFTH

	AUS	IMO	NED	ITA	GBR	USA	ITA	SPA	CZE	GBR	RUS	GER	POR	FRA
Race 1	7	9	R	-	4	4	5	16	R	4	R	R	6	13
Race 2	4	5	1	6	1	2	2	5	12	9	7	4	2	2

2011 WSBK

	Poles	Races	Podiums	Wins	Fastest Laps	Final Pos
Honda	2	18	5	2	0	NINTH

	AUS	GBR	NED	ITA	USA	GER	IMO	FRA	POR
Race 1	12	5	1	6	RET	10	1	RET	3
Race 2	4	6	3	RET	11	4	RET	RET	3

2010 WSBK

	Poles	Races	Podiums	Wins	Fastest Laps	Final Pos
Honda	1	23	10	4	5	FOURTH

	AUS	POR	SPA	NED	ITA	RSA	USA	ITA	CZE	GBR	GER	FRA
Race 1	4	3	6	1	R	5	14	13	1	2	1	12
Race 2	6	R	5	1	R	2	8	12	2	2	2	-

2009 WSBK

Honda	Poles	Races	Podiums	Wins	Fastest Laps	Final Pos
	0	28	8	2	2	FIFTH

	AUS	QAT	SPA	NED	ITA	RSA	USA	ITA	GBR	CZE	GER	IMO	FRA	POR
Race 1	5	12	R	7	5	4	5	7	7	3	4	7	R	2
Race 2	9	8	13	5	4	3	3	1	15	4	1	6	3	3

2008 WSBK

Honda	Poles	Races	Podiums	Wins	Fastest Laps	Final Pos
	0	2	0	0	0	26th

	POR
Race 1	4
Race 2	15

2008 World Supersport

Honda	Poles	Races	Podiums	Wins	Fastest Laps	Final Pos
	0	12	6	3	0	RUNNER-UP

	QAT	AUS	SPA	NED	ITA	GER	ITA	CZE	GBR	GBR	ITA	FRA
Race 1	R	5	6	2	R	6	3	1	1	3	1	10

Key:

AUS = Australia	ITA = Italy	RUS = Russia
CZE = Czech Republic	MAL = Malaysia	SPA = Spain
FRA = France	NED = Holland	THA = Thailand
GBR = Great Britain	POR = Portugal	USA = United States
GER = Germany	QAT= Qatar	
IMO= Imola	RSA = South Africa	

Others

2012 MotoGP Championship – 2 races (Honda RCV213V), finished
    8th and 7th

2007 British Superbike Championship – Runner-up (Honda
    CBR1000RR)

2004 British Supersport Championship (Honda)

2003 British 125cc Championship (Red Bull Rookies Honda)

2003 Arenacross Championship – Winner

1997 British 60cc Motocross Championship (Kawasaki KX60)

1997 Irish and Ulster Motocross Championship

1993 British Youth Motocross Championship, 50cc class

INDEX